IT IS WELL WITH
My Soul

—∼∿∾⌒⚬⚬⌒∾∿∼—

Ninety Days of Reflection

—∼∿∾⌒⚬⚬⌒∾∿∼—

Gods Best to you, and may He Bless you As you Read this

Written by

TOD SALTS

Founder and Senior Pastor
"Salt with a Mission"

ISBN 978-1-64569-031-3 (paperback)
ISBN 978-1-64569-033-7 (hardcover)
ISBN 978-1-64569-032-0 (digital)

Christian Faith Publishing, Inc.
832 Park Avenue
Meadville, PA 16335
www.christianfaithpublishing.com

Printed in the United States of America

Dedicated to Debby Salts.

SALT WITH A MISSION

TOD SALTS

Saltwithamission@aol.com
P.O. Box 794, Tyler, TX 75710

It is Well with My Soul: Ninety Days of Reflection

Including

- Brother Tod's personal journal entries, poems, and stories

- Many of his sermon notes and favorite illustrations

- Ninety days of thought-provoking spiritual truths

- Answers to life's most difficult questions

FOREWORD

Tod Salts is an inspired, ordained minister of God. The devotions in this book reflect God's inspiration and Tod's devoted service to God and God's people. Tod is employed full-time to distribute commercial products to businesses in Texas, Louisiana, Arkansas, and Oklahoma. While accomplishing these responsibilities, he also serves as founding pastor of *Salt with a Mission*. Through this ministry, Tod offers his time and services to spread the Word of God.

He delivers editions of the *American Patriot's Bible* to the women's crisis centers, to family assistance centers, to Wounded Warriors, and other groups and locations. He also provides copies of *Truth for Youth* Bibles, editions of the *American Family Association Journal*, and the Billy Graham Evangelistic Association's publication, *Decision Magazine*. All of which are maintained in over a hundred locations. This outreach includes motels, the employee breakrooms of many, medium to large businesses, as well as other organizations. Tod also spreads the Word through preaching. He leads Bible studies and Sunday worship services at both Oak Hills Terrace and Prestige Estates, in Tyler, Texas.

Tod's goal is to provide God's Word to as many people and places as possible. He is committed to equipping, inspiring and encouraging as many people as he can through teaching, preaching and distributing the Bible. In these devotionals, Tod provides daily inspiration through reflections on Scripture and his experiences in his journey with his Lord and Savior, Jesus Christ. As we said at the beginning, Tod Salts is an inspired minister of God! Through his tireless ministry, he leads others to faith and service to God!

Donald L. Davidson
Professor (retired)
East Texas Baptist University

ACKNOWLEDGMENTS

I want to thank Dr. Donald Davidson for his continued encouragement over the years. I was honored to have him write the forward to this book. Dr. Davidson served in the Pentagon as chair of the Armed Forces Chaplains Board, in the Office of the Secretary of Defense.

Prior to retiring as a full Colonel, Dr. Davidson served two years as clergy to the Secretary of Defense and to the President of the United States, providing advice on religious issues.

Dr. Davidson has a Master of Divinity degree and I was privileged to have studied under him for three and a half years at East Texas Baptist University. His knowledge, encouragement, and friendship have been vital to my overall spiritual growth.

I also owe a great deal of gratitude to my friend, Dex Crosby. His continuous prayers and encouragement have always been inspirational to me. Dex led me in a prayer to receive Jesus as my Lord and Savior over twenty-five years ago. He also taught me to witness. Dex Crosby supports me in the ministry and is my accountability partner and spiritual father to this day. No one has invested more time and energy mentoring me than Dex Crosby.

I would like to thank Bible teachers like David Jeremiah, Tony Evans, Burt Harper, Alex McFarland, Robert Jeffress, and many others who share their knowledge through their preaching and teaching. I have learned a great deal from these men. I have also benefited from the teaching of many great communicators from the past, like, J. Vernon McGee, Adrian Rogers and C.S. Lewis.

I also want to thank the American Family Association, the Family Research Center, and all the faith-based organizations, who stand for faith, family, and freedom. These strong voices of truth helped motivate me to write this book. If it were not for talk radio hosts like Bryan Fischer, Sandy Rios, and Tony Perkins, I would still be uninformed and misinformed concerning the issues that we face as a nation.

However, the person responsible for seeing this project come to completion is the same person who gives me purpose every single day, His name is Jesus Christ. Without Him, I could not have done any of this. My drive, my will, my passion and my motivation to see this through all stem from God's active involvement in my daily life. Therefore, I humbly submit to you that Jesus was the author of this book, and that I am the co-author.

Finally, I want to thank my wife, Debby Salts. Debby has always shared in my desire to see this project come to fruition. I invested a lot of time and effort working on this project. In addition, my job kept me from home two or three days at a time. The many years I spent writing and rewriting, what started out as a 356-day devotional/discipleship manual, ultimately became the book you are holding in your hands. I don't ever remember Debby complaining. She has always encouraged me when it comes to the ministry. I believe her sacrifices have been just as vital as my own during the writing of this book.

A few years ago, Debby began to have trouble walking, and she began to fall on occasion. Her illness progressed, and it was discovered that she had foot drop, a gait abnormality due to weakness or paralysis. A customized prosthetic was made for her right foot. But her mobility continued to decline. We saw many doctors and we were deeply troubled because we were still waiting on a diagnosis. On May 1, 2017, Debby was diagnosed with ALS (Lou Gehrig's Disease). ALS kills the body's motor neurons, systematically paralyzing every muscle in the body until patients lose their ability to walk, talk, eat and eventually breathe. Unlike many paraplegic patients with spinal injuries, people with ALS can still feel pain. Today, there is no cure and the life expectancy is only 2-5 years. Her diagnosis came about the same time I was finishing up my work on this book.

I knew very little about ALS, but I do know firsthand what it is doing to Debby. My heart aches as I watch the progression of this disability, and sometimes I feel so helpless. I want to fix things, I even asked God to allow me to go through this for her, but God has made it clear that He wants me to go through it with her. I have prayed, and I will continue to pray that God will heal Debby. I don't know the number of days God has predetermined for her, and sometimes it is difficult for me to pray the words, "Not my will, but Thine." For this reason, I planned to name this book, *Not My Will.* However, something happened that caused me to change my mind. One day last year, Debby asked me to buy her a necklace. The front side of it had the words, "It is Well" and the other side had the words, "With My Soul." I was overwhelmed with emotion when I realized the extent of Debby's faith. Not only had Debby accepted God's will to be done, she had taken it a step further. The truth is, I had a harder time telling God that things were well with my soul than I did praying the words, "Not my will, but Thine." Oh, I was willing to accept God's decision, but I wasn't ready to say I was okay with it. It hasn't been easy, but today, I can honestly say, "It is well with my soul." For this reason, I changed the name of the book to, *It is Well with My Soul.*

We have been married for thirty-three years, and we have never been closer than we are today. In fact, the past ten years have been the best years of my life. In all our years together, I don't recall a foul word ever coming from her mouth. She is a gem among ladies, an example of godly integrity, and a blessing to me. Over the past decade, I learned how to embrace God's love. And by His Grace, I have learned to love Him back. And in the process, I learned how to love my wife with the kind of love God expects of me.

None of this would be possible without the love of a good woman. I realize that God may be calling her home sooner than I would like. But only God knows when our time here on earth will end. Perhaps she will outlive me. Having said that, it is extremely difficult to imagine going through life without her.

I would like to take this opportunity to say:

> Thank you, Debby. Thank you for being you. Thank you for making me want to be a better man. Thank you for taking me to church all

those years ago. I will always love you. Next to God, no one has had a greater influence in my life than you. If I could travel back in time and pick any woman from any generation to be my wife, I would choose you again.

You loved me when others considered me unlovable. And I thank God every day for the time we have had together. The doctors say your condition is terminal, but I want you to know that my love for you is eternal. God brought us together all those years ago, for such a time as this. And I want you to know, you give me purpose every day and that I am truly humbled to be part of one of what I consider to be the greatest love stories ever told.

Isn't it ironic that I am caring for the one who took care of me and the kids for so many years?

And believe me when I say, it is an honor and a privilege to care for you during this difficult time in your life. And if we live to be one hundred, I will be there by your side, taking care of you. I'm sure you would do the same for me. God is teaching me to appreciate and to embrace the motherly instinct that you were born with. And to be honest, this experience has brought me closer to God. This chapter in our life is teaching me the true meaning of sacrificial and unconditional love.

I pray that you will be here to see this book published, because it would not have been written if God had not given you to me in holy matrimony. For this reason, I dedicate this book to you!

Day 1

It wasn't long after praying to receive Jesus as his savior that a certain man recognized a calling to the ministry. For many years, he strived to live up to his calling. But he was inconsistent at best. The person he disappointed the most was himself. Numerous times, he failed to live up to his commitments.

The main cause of these failed commitments can be attributed to an addiction to alcohol. He was in serious bondage to alcohol, and he knew it. He loved his family with all his heart and the thought of losing them was unbearable. So he usually started his day with good intentions, but, more often than not, he found himself giving in to the temptation to drink. He would say and do things when he drank that brought shame, pain, and suffering to himself and his family. He did not like himself when he drank—and neither did anyone else.

After receiving his second DUI, he almost threw in the towel. However, like so many times before, he found the strength to sober up and try again. He was what some people refer to as a functioning alcoholic. He would stay sober when he had to work, and he *was* a hard worker. Unfortunately, as time went by, he fell deeper and deeper into depression. And every time he fell off the wagon, it was worse than the time before.

Every time he drank he pleaded with God to let him die. In his mind, he was of little use to God; he was a man without purpose. Therefore, life to him was not worth living. When He prayed for death, he prayed it would come during a time of sobriety. He was tired of dragging God's name through the mud and tired of living the life of a hypocrite. He was sick and tired of being sick and tired!

But try as he might, victory in Christ eluded him. He had struggled with this addiction since he was a teenager, and he was at the end of his rope. He used alcohol to self-medicate when his back gave him trouble, and he used it when he felt like no one cared. He used it when he was happy, and he used it when he was sad. He always had an excuse to drink.

There were many times during and after a relapse that he considered suicide. He played out dozens of scenarios in his mind concerning the method he would use to kill himself. But he always found a reason not to go through with it. Something inside him would not allow it. That something, was *someone*, and that someone was Jesus.

When he was sober, he pleaded with God, not to give up on him and that he would not give up on himself. The remorse he felt and the tears he shed during these prayers were immeasurable, but his addiction seemed insurmountable. Knowing he had a calling to the ministry only added to the pain and guilt that he was living with. And the death wishes kept resurfacing.

He had a friend and mentor by the name of Rick Forrest. At one time, Rick was the outreach leader of the Church that he attended. Together they had witnessed to many people and led some of these people in a prayer to receive Jesus as their Lord and Savior.

One day while traveling for work, he received a phone call telling him that his friend Rick had passed away. Rick's death was difficult for him to accept. It became even more difficult when he learned that alcohol played a role in his friend's death. Over the next few weeks, all he could think about was the death of his friend. He didn't want to die like Rick did, so he continuously cried out to God with every fiber of his being: "God, please don't let me go down the same road Rick Forrest went down!" For nearly four weeks he echoed these words.

Then a new client was added to his customer base. When he glanced at the account information, the first thing he noticed was that it was in Forrest City, Arkansas. His mind was continuously thinking about his friend Rick Forrest, and now he was driving to a town called Forrest City. He shrugged this off as a mere coincidence. But when he took a closer look at the route book, he couldn't help but cry. The address of this new account was on 201 Dead Rick Road. The street and the city mimicked what he had been begging God to avoid.

For years he had cried out to the Lord with all his heart, mind, and soul, and nothing significant happened. Now God had done something beyond explanation. This could not be interpreted as a mere coincidence. It was like one of those miracles people read about but never experience.

When he considered the timing and everything else that God had to do to bring this miracle to completion, he was deeply moved. He began to understand that God went to all this trouble just for him. Because of this, he experienced God's love in an entirely new way. He began to see God in all His holiness and righteousness. And in seeing God like this, he knew that he could no longer live in a lifestyle of habitual sin.

God deserved so much more, so he vowed to give God what He deserved. His life began to take on new meaning. Soon he quit drinking altogether and completely surrendered his life to God. From that point on, he was no longer in control of his life, Jesus was. His life was no longer about him. An addiction would never again define him because his life became all about glorifying God.

I believe the odds of winning the lottery are better than this happening by chance. You may ask, "How do I know that this story is true?" I know this story is true because I am the man in the story! God has had me on the fast track ever since this miracle happened. Every three months I go back to 201 Deadrick Road, in Forrest City Arkansas. And every time I go, I am reminded of the road I once frequented, a road cluttered with failed commitments, heartache, shame and disappointment. And then, just like that, I am reminded of the road that I now travel: a road prepared by and paved by God.

In retrospect, I don't think I really wanted to die; I believe I wanted to die to the sin nature. I just did not know how to articulate it at the time. Fortunately, God granted my request based upon on my heart and not my words.

Romans 8:23 says, "The Spirit helps us in our weakness; for we do not know how to pray as we should, but the Spirit Himself intercedes for us with groanings too deep for words." However, it is true that I had to die before I could start living. My sinful lifestyle, my will, my pride, and my disposition, all these things had to die, if I was to truly live for Jesus. I have had to be willing to unlearn everything I thought I knew, and I have been happy to do it.

In order that you could see what I saw that day, I have included a snapshot of the actual route sheet that God used to get my attention.

2800 SOUTH HAZEL ST.	PINE BLUFF, AR	# 102
2721 SOUTH CAMDEN RD.	PINE BLUFF, AR	# 103
5805 DOLLARWAY RD	PINE BLUFF, AR	# 104
201 DEADRICK ROAD	FORREST CITY, AR	# 1813
2808 LAKEWOOD VILLAGE DR	N LITTLE ROCK, AR	# 0374
2602 CANTRELL ROAD	LITTLE ROCK, AR	# 3215
4220 E. MCCAIN BLVD.	LITTLE ROCK, AR	# 313
105 GREGORY PLAZA DR	JACKSONVILLE,AR	# 0553
6020 JOHN F KENNEDY BLVD	LITTLE ROCK, AR	# 1575

I think of Rick often. He was used by God to help me in a significant way during his life. Amazingly, he continues to do so even after his death. The positive impact he has had on my life is apparent to everyone who knows me. I know in my heart that the Lord used my friend, Rick Forrest, to display God's divine providence in my own life. And for this I am so very thankful.

Scripture Reference for the Day: "I have been crucified with Christ and I no longer live, but Christ lives in me. The life I now live in the body, I live by faith in the Son of God, who loved me and gave himself for me." (Galatians 2:20)

Day 2

Years ago, I was volunteering with a food ministry in east Texas. Clyde Powell, a friend and retired preacher, helped with the ministry faithfully each week. I had a lot of questions about the Bible and Clyde shared a story about a young man who had similar questions concerning the Bible. Here is my version of that story.

Once upon a time there was a young man who just so happened to be a new Christian. And he had a lot of questions. An elder of the church he attended told him to write all the questions he had down on sticky notes. Then he told the young man to stick the questions to his desk. He said, "As you study the word of God, many of your questions will be answered. When you get an answer to one of your questions, pull that particular sticky note down and throw it away." It wasn't long before he had posted questions all over his desk and his wall.

Over the years he continued to study God's word and eventually many of his questions were answered. When he was an old man at the end of his life, he noticed that there were still three Post-it notes left on his on his desk. He read over the questions and then he threw them away.

He had learned that there were many answers to be found in the Bible, but he also learned that some things were not meant to be understood this side of heaven. Some things need to be accepted by faith.

Like the man in this story, I had a lot of questions about God. During the seven years I spent writing this book, I was on a mission to get answers to my questions. By the grace of God, I was able to find the answers to many of the questions that I had searched for. You will find answers to those questions throughout these pages and much more.

Scripture Reference for the Day: "Now faith is the assurance of things hoped for, the conviction of things not seen." (Hebrews 11:1)

Day 3

Debby and I were married on March 1, 1986. Since then, we have been blessed with two children and three grandchildren.

Nothing blesses me more than having to go back and add another name to our list of grandbabies. We have always loved our children unconditionally and understood that they are a gift from God. In fact, we named our daughters Sarah and Rebekah after women in the Bible.

After the children leave home and parents get a little older, having grandchildren is something looked forward to with great anticipation. We have received a great gift: experiencing what it means to be grandparents. Rebekah and her husband Kenny also used the Bible in the naming of their children.

On December 2, 2009, we were blessed with our first grandchild: Isaac. The Hebrew definition of the name *Isaac* means "to laugh." With Isaac, we received more than just an ability to laugh more often; we learned to laugh even during the most difficult times.

We didn't think our marriage needed any fixing at the time of his birth. But in retrospect, it is easy to see how Isaac brought a sense of oneness to our relationship by giving us a common purpose. His life has not only brought us closer together as a couple, he brought unity to the entire family. Just as laughter is good medicine, so is our grandson Isaac. Proverbs 17:22 says, "Laughter is a good medicine."

On November 5, 2010, we were blessed with another grandchild: a beautiful little girl named Abigail. The Biblical name *Abigail* in Hebrew means "source of joy." And true to her name, Abigail brings joy to all who know her. Happiness is a goal that is seldom sustainable—happiness depends on happenings. But true joy depends on faith. Joy transcends our circumstances every time we see Abigail. She truly is a joy to behold. Jesus said in John 15:11, "I have told you this so that my Joy may be in you and that your Joy may be complete."

On August 15, 2013, we were blessed with a third grandbaby: Selah. The word *Selah* can be found in two books of the Bible, but is most prevalent in the Psalms, where it appears seventy-one times. *Selah* seems to have a combination of meanings, all of them are spiritual in nature. Selah can mean "to meditate, or to reflect on the things of God" as well as "to praise" or "to lift up." I think a good way of defining Selah is as "an Amen with an exclamation point." Our granddaughter Selah, like her siblings, is true to her name. When we see her, we can't help thinking, "Amen!" Her arrival has caused us to consider our many blessings and to magnify and praise God, the Creator of all life. David said in Psalm 32:7, "You are my hiding place; You preserve me from trouble; You surround me with songs of deliverance. Selah."

Next to Jesus, nothing brings more purpose in the life of those who are past their prime than grandchildren. To them, grandchildren are a spiritual experience, and a blessing like no other. As I grow older, I realize that the number of years I live is not nearly as important as the life I live during those years. It is not the length of life, but depth of life that gives purpose.

Therefore, I characterize my grandchildren as a supernatural gift from God. Grandchildren can bring vitality back to a person even after their metabolism has slowed to a crawl. Proverbs 17:6 says, "Grandchildren are the crown of old men." In summary, I believe that grandchildren are God's way of rewarding us grandparents for being faithful to His command to populate the earth.

Scripture Reference for the Day: "God blessed them; and God said to them, 'Be fruitful and multiply, and fill the earth.'" (Genesis 1:28)

Day 4

I have dealt with back problems for many years now. In fact, years ago, prior to surgery and before I knew Jesus, I went through a four-week, pain management clinic. This was a program designed to teach people how to live with chronic pain. The staff taught us specific exercises and techniques to help minimize the pain associated with back injuries. We also participated in some psychological exercises. These sessions were designed to help us relax and cope with the consequences of being injured.

One day they led us into a room and we were told to relax in a recliner. Then they told us to make ourselves as comfortable as possible. The recliner in that room was the most comfortable chair I have ever had the privilege of sitting in. I remember the psychologist turning the lights off and turning on a tape recorder. As I relaxed a gentle, hypnotic voice walked us through a maze that eventually led to a giant wall. My journey did not end there; I had to get over that wall.

I was told that all my dreams would come true if I could just get over that wall. I remember at that point, thinking about the song "Over the Rainbow."

The rest of my journey was up to my imagination. Occasionally, the familiar hypnotic voice would remind me that something special was waiting for me on the other side. I allowed my imagination to go with the program. I soon found out that getting to the other side of that wall was one of the hardest things that I had ever done. I would climb two feet only to slide back one. The higher I climbed, the tougher the task.

The entire time I was having visions of what might be on the other side. I perceived money, gold and all the riches in the world. I perceived fame and luxury that very few ever get the chance to experience. But as I neared the top, I noticed all my strength had been consumed and I knew that I could not get myself over the wall. Suddenly there was an interruption of my imagination. I don't know how I knew this, but I knew that it wasn't my imagination finishing this journey.

I had used every ounce of strength that I had, and I was ready to give up, when I noticed a hand reaching down to help me get over the wall. When I looked up to see whose hand I was holding, I saw a man in a white robe. The hood of His robe covered just enough of his face to hide his identity. But, somehow, I knew it was Jesus. I don't know how I knew it was Him. Perhaps it was a nail-scarred hand that opened my eyes to who He was or perhaps it was God speaking directly to me. Whatever it was, I knew in my heart that it was Jesus in my vision.

It was at this point that all my dreams of fame and fortune were forgotten. Tears filled my eyes as I realized for the first time that Jesus was the answer to all my dreams. What awaited me on the other side no longer mattered, as long as Jesus was there. Suddenly the lights came on and the session was over. I wiped the tears from my eyes and looked around to see if anyone else had tears in their eyes. Perhaps somebody else had seen Jesus too. Or perhaps they found their fame and fortune. I will never know, but what I do know is that before I was saved, I had this very real and memorable encounter with Jesus.

It would be nearly five years later before I finally invited Jesus into my life. In retrospect, I can see how God was preparing me for this very moment in time.

The fact remains, this world can be a very difficult place. Maybe you feel like you don't have the strength to carry on. Or, perhaps you feel as if you are ready to give up. To you I say, "Look up! The same hand that reached down to me is reaching down to you. Jesus is patiently waiting for you to place your trust in Him. Put your hand in the hand of the only begotten Son of God." And when you do, you will discover that dreams really do come true.

Scripture Reference for the Day: "Behold, I stand at the door and knock; if anyone hears My voice and opens the door, I will come in to him and will dine with him, and he with Me." (Revelation 3:20)

Since the day I prayed to receive Jesus, my call to the ministry has been undeniable. But at that time, I was not ready to place myself under the authority of God. Therefore, the sin nature remained prevalent in my life for many years. For the longest time, I thought if I just stayed busy enough doing the Lord's work, I would avoid succumbing to temptation.

I prayed that God would take away my desire to sin. I prayed that God would help me to modify my behavior. But all the while, God just wanted my desires and prayers to be about Him. For years I had focused on my sin rather than the answer to my sin. I spent many years working on my behavior instead of my relationship with God. I had continuously asked for God's help in this, not realizing that I was asking for the wrong things.

Overcoming temptation is not about a person's will power. Overcoming temptation is about a person's faith. It is Christ in us, that gives us the power to overcome the sin nature. The sin problem cannot be eliminated by changing our behavior, because our core problem is internal not external.

Everyday people commit and recommit their allegiance to their God but fall short in fulfilling their commitments to God. Their intentions are good. However, they fail to understand that behavioral modification is something that happens on the outside. And in most cases, it is only a temporary fix. Today I am free from the bondage of sin, not because of anything I did, but because of what Jesus did.

Unfortunately, we do not think in the same way that God thinks. In Isaiah 55:8 God said, "My thoughts are not your thoughts, nor are your ways My ways." Supernatural chains cannot be broken by natural means.

I wanted to be in the ministry—but God wanted *the ministry to be in me*! Once God opened my eyes to the truth, I could no longer live my life in habitual sin. Eventually sinful desires were no longer my focus. God had given me a new heart with new desires. It is amazing how everything changes when your priorities change. My desire to be in ministry had previously been the driving force behind the Kingdom work I did. Today, honoring Jesus Christ is the motivation behind everything I do for the Kingdom.

I knew that I had to find ways to share my story so that others might see the importance of surrendering to God. Since then I have been trying to convey to anyone who will listen, the importance of surrendering over to God, all your heart, mind and soul. I want everyone to experience the freedom that comes from this. I am not talking about committing to God. I was committed to God for years. Anybody can make a commitment to themselves, to others, and even to their God. The problem with commitment is this: when we make commitments, we are in control over whether we follow through with them.

This is why so many believers fail to follow through with their commitments. But when we surrender, it's a different story all together. When we surrender, we give control of our lives to the person that we surrender to. For example, when a soldier surrenders to his enemy, he is taken captive. He gives up any control he had previously. His life is in the hands of his enemy.

But when we surrender our life over to God, the opposite happens. We are set free from the bondage of sin, thereby, free to live for Christ. Romans 8:2 says, "For in Christ Jesus the law of the Spirit of life has set you free from the law of sin and death." And in Romans 8:36 it says, "So if the Son sets you free, you will be free indeed." I am happy to say that I am no longer in control of my life, I have been set free!

I gave control of my life over to Jesus when I surrendered my all to Him. Today, I base my decisions on what God wants and not on what I want. Today, I do not just follow Jesus, I walk with Him.

The relief I have, knowing that sinful choices are no longer mine to make, gives me a peace I never knew. It is truly a peace that surpasses understanding. And the best part is the sense of restored innocence this entails.

Once a person experiences this peace and the freedom that comes from allowing God to reign, he will never go back to a sinful life style. But until a person elevates Jesus to His proper place, he will be unwilling and unable to give all of himself to his God. In addition, he will be subject to the sin nature and held captive by it until he is ready to surrender. Every person is either subject to the sin nature, or subject to God. Consider Matthew 6:24: "No one can serve two masters; for either he will hate the one and love the other, or he will be devoted to one and despise the other."

I ask you, "Is Jesus the Lord over your thoughts; is He the Lord over your mouth? Is Jesus the Lord over your time?" If He isn't, He should be. As believers, we belong to Him. Jesus paid a great price to ransom our souls from the fires of Hell, and we owe it to Him to be obedient to His will. Second Corinthians 5:15 says, "And he died for all, so that those who live should no longer live for themselves but for him who died for them and was raised again." Surrendering to Christ should be the last independent decision that you ever make.

Scripture Reference for the Day: "Do you not know that your body is a temple of the Holy Spirit who is in you, whom you have received from God? You are not your own; you were bought at a price. Therefore, honor God with your bodies." (1 Corinthians 6:19, 20)

Day 6

For forgiveness to take place, we must go to God in repentance. But for true repentance to take place we need to agree with God concerning our sin. We must call sin what it is.

One day a pastor spoke out strongly against sin during a church service. His goal was to steer the congregation away from sin by explaining the serious consequences that follow sin. Later that day some of the church members went to the minister's house. They shared their concern that some people were offended by the pastor's straightforward approach toward sin. They asked him not to talk so bluntly about sin in the future. They even went so far as to ask him to consider using the word mistake, rather than the word sin. They said they were concerned that his approach could cause the younger people to stop coming to church.

The minister excused himself and walked out to the shed. A few minutes later he returned holding a bottle with the word "POISON" written in large capital letters on the label. Then he said to the people, "I understand where you're coming from. But I do not think you understand what you are asking. You want me to change this label. Suppose I take this poison label off, and suppose I replace it with a milder less-threatening label. What if I changed this label to say, *CANDY* instead of poison? Can you not see the danger in this?"

For decades we have been putting a milder label on sin. This trend has gotten worse over time and today even the word *sin* is considered "politically incorrect" by a large percent of the population.

Rafael Cruz, the father of Senator Ted Cruz of Texas, said it best when he said, "Instead of being politically correct, we need to become biblically correct." Even the concept of sin has been watered down to the point that many Americans no longer consider what God says to be sin, sin.

It is high time that we put a *POISON* label back on the poison bottle. We should be just as serious about sin as God is. Make no mistake, sin is a poison, and the milder the label that is placed on it, the deadlier the poison becomes.

Scripture Reference for the Day: "Therefore, just as through one man, sin entered into the world, and death through sin, and so death spread to all men, because all sinned." (Romans 5:12)

Day 7

America is changing—good is being called evil and evil is being exalted. Political correctness is trumping God's word and the Constitution. Righteousness is being overruled. A new ideology is erasing rationality to the point where truth and facts no longer matter.

We must recognize that we have enemies, like the Freedom from Religion Foundation who has set out to literally remove any aspect of God from our culture. When God is removed from a civilized culture, the end result will always be chaos and anarchy. Proverbs 14:34 says, "Righteousness exalts a nation, but sin condemns any people."

These anti-Christian groups are organized and very well-funded. They use bully tactics to force schools, businesses, and individuals to bow a knee to their anti-God agenda. They claim constitutional authority, even though the Constitution does not support their claims. But there is a light at the end of the tunnel. In nearly every case where Christians stood their ground, we prevailed in the end.

Many of these groups claim that Christian beliefs and ideas are offensive and therefore, are unconstitutional threats. Yet the constitution does not give anyone the right not to be offended. But this is how proponents of political correctness think. They know they cannot win the debate, so they use their freedom of speech to silence the freedom of speech of those they disagree with.

Every freedom we have hinges on the freedom of religion. And we are very close to losing this liberty.

The Christian walk is not based upon an opinion—it is all about God's truth. If you hold any opinion that runs contrary to God's word, then obviously God is not your ultimate authority. We do not stand on what we think to be true—we stand on what God *says* to be true! We are just the messengers.

As a person grows in their faith, it become less about what he thinks and more about what he knows. I expect the lost to behave like lost people. But the thing I don't understand is how Christians can try to justify their silence by saying that they don't get involved in politics.

Authentic Christians have always been countercultural. Dietrich Bonhoeffer famously said, "Silence in the face of evil is itself evil: God will not hold us guiltless." Jesus and His disciples were not silent, and neither should we be silent.

When Jesus walked the earth, the Jewish community's legislative system was led by a group known as the Sanhedrin. The Sanhedrin was a council of seventy-one leaders with one chief justice and one vice-chief justice. It was a mixture of scribes, Sadducees and Pharisees. The legislators were not elected by the people, and the judicial and legislative branches were combined into one branch.

The Roman government gave the Sanhedrin the authority and power to rule over the Jewish community. This was a way by which the people could be controlled. These Jewish leaders were just like modern-day politicians. The only real difference between them and the politicians today is two thousand years of history.

By condemning these leaders and revealing the truth about who they were, Jesus shook up the system. In fact, He spoke out strongly against them on multiple occasions. Jesus was a threat to their positions of authority. For this reason, they became the driving force behind the crucifixion. Speaking out against the Sanhedrin back then, was considered unacceptable, just as Christians talking about politics today is considered unacceptable.

Jesus was definitely very involved in the political culture of His day. John the Baptist was beheaded because he spoke out against the sexual immorality of King Herod. If that was not political, I don't know what is. Consider for a moment what Jesus said about John the Baptist. In Matthew 11:11, Jesus said, "Truly I tell you, among those born of women there has not risen anyone greater than John the Baptist."

Being involved in the Lord's work requires Christians to get involved in the culture. If this is political, so be it! Jesus is our example and He was deeply engaged in cultural issues. What we call political today was considered spiritual by our forefathers. What society calls political are spiritual in the eyes of God. All the world's problems are spiritual. Ray Comfort wisely said, "This is not a God-forsaken world, it is a world that has forsaken God."

Ecclesiastes says, "There's nothing new under the sun." The values portrayed in Scripture are no different than those our Founding Fathers lived by and died for. And they are the same values that we promise to uphold every time we go to church and participate in praise and worship services.

Scripture Reference for the Day: "Therefore put on the full armor of God, so that when the day of evil comes, you may be able to stand your ground, and after you have done everything, to stand. Stand firm." (Ephesians 6:13)

In a sermon, the late J. Vernon McGee compared the coming of Christ to that of a man becoming an ant. I have always been intrigued by that analogy. I have had to deal with ants in my yard much like Dr. McGee did in his. The only difference is, the ants in my yard are fire ants. And when these little pests bite you, you know you've been bitten. These ants would take over my property if I didn't do everything I could to stop them. I use poison every year to keep them out of the house and out of the yard.

I don't get any enjoyment from killing any of God's creatures. And If I could communicate with the ant, I would try to explain my situation in order that they might find another place to live. I would explain to them that there is a big world out there with plenty of room for them and their families. I would explain that by leaving they could live in peace.

But to communicate with the ants I would have to become an ant. A man becoming an ant would make a great story. However, I don't think I would be willing to become an ant, go into enemy territory, and reveal my identity. I am sure they would kill me. Hey, wait a minute, this sounds an awful lot like what happened to Jesus, doesn't it?

Yes, a man becoming an ant would be a significant undertaking. However, God becoming a man—now that is something to write home about! Man becoming an ant is one created creature becoming another created creature. But for God to become a man, the Creator had to become the created. There is a difference of gigantic proportions in these two scenarios.

Jesus got down on our level, so he could communicate to us. God knew He had to reveal Himself to us in an understandable way. Therefore, Jesus became flesh and blood, just like you and me. God did this, so He could be understood by His creation.

Romans 8:3 says, "For what the law was powerless to do because it was weakened by the flesh, God did by sending his own Son in the likeness of sinful flesh to be a sin offering. And so he condemned sin in the flesh."

Let me summarize this by saying, "Christ became one of us, so we could see what God is like and relate to Him." In doing so, Jesus offered a solution for our trespasses by offering Himself as the final sacrifice for sin. Jesus is immortal, therefore, becoming human was the only way He could die. The immortal became mortal to save us from our sin.

Words cannot begin to explain how humbling it must have been for the Creator to become the created.

Why did He do it? Why did Jesus come in the flesh, knowing, that he would be hated and killed? The answer is quite simple. He loved us. God created man in His own image, and He holds great value in all human life. Indeed, to God every human life is precious. In fact, the Word of God teaches us that we are the most valued commodity in all His creation.

Jesus loved us enough to die for us. And all He asks for in return is that we love Him back. Have you loved Him back? Jesus said, "If you love Me you will obey My word." Do you love God enough to walk in obedience to His word?

Scripture Reference for the Day: "If you love Me, you will keep My commandments." (John 14:15)

Day 9

When I heard a comparison of God's love to that of a new mother's love on the radio program *Exploring the Word*, I was immediately compelled to write it down. Understanding the love we have for our own children is a great way for us to begin understanding God's love for us. When a woman gives birth to her first child, she discovers new insight into what love really is. She has never experienced anything this deep and this meaningful. She wonders how she could ever love anyone as much as she loves her little baby.

In fact, her love runs so deep that she feels as if every ounce of love that she possesses is wrapped up in that one child. A few years later she has another baby. She loves the second child just as much as she did the first one. Then she has a third baby, and she loves that child just as much as she does the first and second child. But here is the amazing part: the love she has for the first and second child never diminishes even though every ounce of her love is being poured into the newborn. Love has no limits! She could have a hundred children and the result would be the same. She would give all her love to every child because the more she loves, the more love she has to give.

Burt Harper said it this way, "Love never diminishes because someone suddenly ran out of love."

This kind of love is not natural—it is supernatural. It is evidence of our being created in the image of God. Anything other than love will diminish when we run out of resources. But love is the one thing that we can never get enough of and by the same token, never run out of. Love defies logic. Love is eternal. First John 4:8 says, "Whoever does not love does not know God, because God is love." God is love and His love for you can never diminish. In fact, God's love goes far beyond the love of a new mother. This side of Heaven, we cannot fully understand the magnitude of God's love for us. I think Jerry Falwell came close when he said, "Love is a commitment to meet another person's needs." True love involves meeting the greatest needs of others. When discussing this subject on *Exploring the Word*, McFarland said, "Our greatest need is to be in a personal relationship with our heavenly Father." Jesus demonstrated His love for us when He died to make that relationship possible.

Scripture Reference for the Day: "For I am convinced that neither death nor life, neither angels nor demons, neither the present nor the future, nor any powers, neither height nor depth, nor anything else in all creation, will be able to separate us from the love of God that is in Christ Jesus our Lord." (Romans 8:38, 39)

Day 10

A very wise man said, "The Bible may hurt you with the truth, but it will never comfort you with a lie." Many people today believe that biblical morality offends people. But if the truth be told, it is the people speaking on God's behalf that are usually offended and hurt. Nothing hurts worse than persecuting words coming from fellow believers.

Persecution from the lost should be expected because they don't know any better. On the other hand, Christians should be defending each other as they defend God's word. Sometimes, when I feel like I have been unfairly condemned by a brother or sister, I share my soul with God. I do this by writing out my innermost feelings. I am always amazed how much better I feel after writing to Jesus. This practice helps me to vent and allows God to reveal how I could have approached a situation in a more Christlike manner. God also uses this time to equip me and to help me better articulate a biblical worldview.

My desire is to be able to articulate truth with love and to do so without watering down the word of God. Anyone who is actively pursuing God will affirm this is not an easy task.

Jesus was crucified for speaking truth and for standing against the authorities of His day. All but two of the original Apostles were martyred for speaking truth. The truth that contradicted the leaders of their day is the same truth we seek to proclaim today. And that is this: The Word of God is inerrant.

Speaking truth is not passing judgment; speaking the truth is an attempt to save others from judgment. I don't write these things to point my finger at anyone or to gain a vote of sympathy from those who might be offended by my words. What I do, I do to glorify God. However, I do have a strong desire for others to understand why I am the way I am, and why I say and do the things I say and do.

How about you? Are you willing to live for Christ? If you had to make the choice, would you die a martyr's death? If you answered yes to this and you have not unconditionally surrendered to God, you may be deceiving yourself. Most people are not willing to die for someone that they are not first willing to live for.

If you want direction in your life, give God your whole heart. God will give you the passion you need to accomplish His will and He will direct your path. But this requires dedication and discipline on the part of the believer. You cannot give God all your heart and at the same time leave your options open. When we leave our options open, we leave the door of sin open. We might fool ourselves but there is no fooling God.

Scripture Reference for the Day "Trust in the LORD with all your heart and do not lean on your own understanding. In all your ways acknowledge Him, And He will make your paths straight." (Proverbs 3:5, 6)

Day 11

Dr. David Jeremiah told a story about a time when he and his wife attended a prayer breakfast where he was to be the guest of honor. During the event, it was brought to his attention that a man attending the breakfast wanted to talk to him. The man looked like he had lived a hard life. He had long red hair with a ponytail that went all the way down his back. His face showed signs that he had aged before his time.

After talking to him, the pastor realized that this man had indeed lived a hard life. The man went on to tell Dr. Jeremiah that he got depressed to the point that he wanted to die, and he was seriously considering suicide. Every day on his way to work, he would drive around this curve; he knew that if he just missed that turn, it would mean certain death.

One morning he made the decision to miss the curve and drive off the cliff. He turned on his radio to his favorite rock-and-roll station, turned the volume up all the way as he prepared to put an end to his journey in life.

But for some reason on that day, the radio wasn't working right. He got angry and hit the dashboard above the radio as hard as he could. When he did this the radio program *Turning Point* with Dr. David Jeremiah came on. He said that the pastor talked about God's great love, His mercy, forgiveness, and grace. And then he said Dr. Jeremiah made it personal when he explained how these things were available to him.

He turned the ignition off, and right there, in the front seat of his car he received Jesus Christ as his personal Lord and Savior. This same man is now serving as a missionary. He chose not only to live, but to live for Christ. Today he lives life with a purpose. Perhaps you are struggling and having a difficult time determining God's purpose for your life. Perhaps you or someone you know is in that dark place and wanting to end it all. If you are stuck in any of these situations, let me say this: God has a plan for you; God has a purpose for your life. God loves you and He wants to forgive you, so you can fulfill the purpose He has for you.

Is not finding purpose every person's desire in life? God will give you the desires of your heart by making you aware of those hidden desires.

All you have to do is give God control of your life by asking Jesus into your heart. Ask Jesus to forgive you and to become the Lord over your life today. Confession plus repentance equals forgiveness. Forgiveness means salvation through Jesus Christ. I promise that you will be glad you did this, and you will never want to go back to your previous life style.

Scripture Reference for the Day: "Delight yourself in the LORD; and He will give you the desires of your heart." (Psalms 34:7)

Day 12

When I was a young child. I remember getting a knife out of a kitchen drawer and cutting up a bar of soap in the bathroom sink. I don't remember why I did it; maybe I was trying to carve something out of the soap. Unfortunately, I forgot to clean up my mess and left everything in the sink.

When my mom confronted me, I lied and said, "It wasn't me." My mom knew that my little brother was too young to have done this, so she continued to question me, and I continued to proclaim my innocence.

That night when I went to bed, I was convicted of my sin in a way that I had never experienced before. We were not raised in church; however, my mom did believe in God. Her belief was no doubt a starting point for me and my faith. However, this doesn't explain how I knew that God was aware of everything I said and did. And an even greater mystery is why I believed these things with every fiber of my being. Somehow, I knew that I was ultimately accountable to God.

That night as I laid in bed, I told God how sorry I was for the lie I told my mom. I was old enough to count to one hundred, so I made up my mind to tell God I was sorry one hundred times. I whispered, "I'm sorry, God" repeatedly. I was determined because I thought that God would surely forgive me if I asked Him one hundred times.

I do not remember reaching my goal. I fell asleep asking God for forgiveness that night. But as I grew up, I began to ignore that little voice that previously compelled me ask God for forgiveness.

The most difficult thing a person can do is accept the fact that they have lost their innocence. And as a young adult, I wasn't about to admit that I had lost mine. But I knew deep down, that was exactly what was happening to me. And every time I ignored that quiet little voice that said, "God is watching you," the easier it was to ignore it the next time.

If we ignore the Holy Spirit's prompting over an extended period, our ability to discern right from wrong begins to deteriorate. Eventually we can lose the ability to recognize it at all. And because of this, I spent years rebelling against God without even knowing that I was doing it. That little boy who cut up the soap was much wiser than that young adult who rarely thought about God.

When my children were born, and my life was no longer just about me, I slowly began to recognize that tiny, quiet voice again. But, because it caused me to see myself as ungodly and rebellious, I purposely ignored it. In fact, I didn't ask Jesus into my heart until I was thirty years old. And it wasn't until I was in my mid-forties that I began to confront sin with the same passion and determination that little boy did so many years ago.

Scripture Reference for the Day: "If we confess our sins, He is faithful and righteous to forgive us our sins and to cleanse us from all unrighteousness." (1 John 1:9)

Day 13

My wife Debby's battle with Lou Gehrig's disease becomes apparent every time she tries to do the simplest of tasks. If God doesn't intervene soon we know that her fight to remain mobile will become a fight for survival.

She currently uses a walker to get around the house. At night, when she makes her way to the bedroom, she must go around to the left side of the bed. With great difficulty, she scoots onto the bed into a position where she can comfortably sleep. Moving toward the center of the bed is very difficult for her because she has lost most of her strength in her right leg and she has foot drop in the right foot.

One night I was asleep when I felt her arm around me. I was surprised to see her on my side of the bed, so I turned to her and asked, "How did you get over here?" It was obvious to me that Debby had used a lot of energy to get there, when she whispered, "It just takes me a while." Debby just needed to be held, so I laid there on my back holding the love of my life in my arms as she rested her head on my chest. As I held her, I began to pray silently in my mind, just as I had done so many other times in the past. And like so many times before, I asked God to heal Debby of this dreadful disease. As I prayed, I began to cry on the inside. My words to God went something like this, "Haven't I been faithful to you Lord? For the last ten years, I have tried to do everything that you have asked of me. Please Lord, heal Debby, heal her in the name of your son, Jesus Christ, I beg of you, heal her."

Then, for some reason, I spoke to Debby. And I began to sob as I choked out these words, "Please don't leave me, Debby. Please don't die."

Debby didn't say anything. What could she say? She just held me as I wept. What started out with me holding her, became a special moment of both of us holding each other. God very gently reminded me that I would never be good enough to move Him to do something. The only righteousness I bring in this life is the righteousness of Christ that was freely given to me. And it is not because of anything I have done, but because of what Jesus did on the cross for me. And realizing just how unworthy I really was made this special moment even more special. I believe what we experienced that night was not only the two of us holding each other, but Jesus holding us, as we held each other. God did not heal Debby that night. But I will never forget the peace that came over me that night. The peace I experienced surpassed human understanding. I know in my heart that God is the one who comforted us that night. I pray that you too will experience this peace, because there is nothing else quite like it this side of heaven.

Author's note: This entry was written in August of 2017. Since then the disease has continued to progress. Today, Debby has been moved to her own room across the hall. She sleeps in a special hospital bed and uses a ventilator to help her breath while she sleeps. I check in on her several times every night. But I will never forget the night, and I will treasure it as long as I live, because it was the last time we were able to hold each other in that way.

Scripture Reference for the Day: "Do not be anxious about anything, but in every situation, by prayer and petition, with thanksgiving, present your requests to God. And the peace of God, which transcends all understanding, will guard your hearts and your minds in Christ Jesus." (Philippians 4:6, 7)

Day 14

The word *sin* appears in the Bible over two thousand times. Sin, by definition, is any failure to conform to God's law or to miss the mark. Sin is the cancer of the universe and we see it manifested every day in our actions and our attitudes.

When Adam and Eve first sinned, blood sacrifices were instituted. In the Old Testament, God allowed for the blood sacrifice of animals to cover the sins of His people. Animals were used because they were innocent of any sin. Animals were not created in the image of God; they live out their lives based on either instinct or training. They do not understand sin and repentance.

Therefore, the animal sacrifice was only a temporary atonement for the sins of man. But it did point to a future blood sacrifice that would last for all eternity. In fact, the entire Old Testament foreshadows the future sacrifice of Christ.

According to the Bible (and medical science), blood is the essence of life. Leviticus 17:11 says, "For the life of the body is in its blood. I have given you the blood on the altar to purify you, making you right with the LORD. It is the blood, given in exchange for a life, that makes purification possible." When a person's skin is cut, their blood begins working to cleanse the wound. A scab forms from the dried blood, sealing and protecting the wound. In a similar way, when we receive Christ as our Lord and Savior, our soul is cleansed by the precious blood Jesus shed on the cross. The cleansing of the soul is required of anyone wanting to enter the Kingdom of Heaven. Immediately upon receiving Christ, the Spirit of God—the Holy

Spirit—comes into us and begins to heal our heart, mind, and soul. And we are sealed by the Spirit of God for all eternity.

2nd Corinthians 1:22 says, "He anointed us, set his seal of ownership on us, and put his Spirit in our hearts as a deposit, guaranteeing what is to come." Ephesians 1:13 says, "When you believed, you were marked in him with a seal, the promised Holy Spirit." And in John 10:29, Jesus said, "My Father, who has given them to me, is greater than all; no one can snatch them out of my Father's hand." The prophets foretold of a future redeemer who would come to save humanity from their sins. Moses, David and every other follower of God in the Old Testament were saved by the future sacrifice of Christ on the cross. Those born after the crucifixion and resurrection are saved by the past sacrifice of Christ on the cross. Nonetheless, it is the same sacrifice, the same blood, the same cross and the same Savior that offers all of humanity a permanent solution to the sin problem. The sacrifice had to be justified in order to justify the sinner. Only the blood of a sinless man would suffice. Only the blood of Jesus Christ, the only begotten Son of God, could save us from our sins. Jesus was and is that sacrifice. The plan of salvation has been, and will always be, Jesus Christ. He alone deserves all the glory honor and praise from every human. One day every knee will bow in honor of our great King. One day Jesus will receive the eternal praise and worship He deserves.

Scripture Reference for the Day: "Blessed is the one whose sin the Lord will never count against them." (Romans 4:8)

Day 15

In today's culture, passing the buck has become as common as a handshake. Years ago, a comedian named Flip Wilson popularized the phrase, "The devil made me do it." But that is not where the phrase originated. In the Garden of Eden, God told Adam and Eve, "You cannot eat from the tree of knowledge of good and evil, for in the day that you eat from it you shall surely die." They both disobeyed God and ate the fruit from the tree. When confronted by God, Adam passed the buck to Eve. Eve, in turn, passed the buck onto Satan. It is safe to surmise that it was Eve and not Flip Wilson who coined the phrase, "The devil made me do it."

We are all looking for someone to blame. We are just like Adam and Eve in that we don't want to be responsible for our own behavior. Adam and Eve started the tradition of passing the buck, and we've kept it going ever since. In Truman's Presidential Library there is an exact reproduction of his old White House office. On Truman's desk sits a sign that has been in the library since 1957. The sign simply says, "The Buck Stops Here."

For years I wondered why the thousand-year reign of Christ was necessary. I thought God should just put an end to Satan. But the Bible says Satan will be released after one thousand years to lead an army in one final attempt to overthrow God. The story of Adam and Eve opened my eyes and answered this question that had been on my mind for so long.

Satan will be bound during Christ's thousand-year reign. However, the sin nature will remain until after the millennial period is over. Therefore, I am convinced that the thousand-year reign of

Christ was predetermined to show humanity that we are responsible for our own sin. Moreover, when the millennial period is over, there will be a multitude of people ready to follow Satan in a final attempt to over throw Jesus. Life will go on, and children will be born during this period in history, and sin will continue to be a problem. Therefore, after the thousand-year reign, no one will be able to use the excuse, "The devil made me do it!" God will prove once and for all why every person must be held responsible for their own sin. Those who reject Jesus will be without excuse. Romans 1:20 says, "For since the creation of the world God's invisible qualities—his eternal power and divine nature—have been clearly seen, being understood from what has been made, so that people are without excuse."

Scripture Reference for the Day: "The man said, 'The woman whom You gave to be with me, she gave me from the tree, and I ate.' Then the LORD God said to the woman, 'What is this you have done?' And the woman said, 'The serpent deceived me, and I ate.' (Genesis 3:12, 13)

Day 16

Have you ever used any of these phrases: "a broken heart," "a wolf in sheep's clothing," "the blind leading the blind," "the powers that be," "go the extra mile," "an eye for an eye and a tooth for a tooth?" The common denominator of all these sayings is God's word. There are hundreds of sayings we use daily that originated from the Scriptures. Most of the time we don't even realize that we are quoting the Bible when we say them.

Today I want to focus on the word *scapegoat*. It caught my attention while reading chapter 16 in the book of Leviticus. The term *scapegoat* is used when an innocent person takes the blame (or is blamed) for something of which they are not guilty. When the people of Israel were wandering in the wilderness, God commanded they set aside one day each year as the Day of Atonement.

On this day, the priest would make a special sacrifice for the sins of all the people. He would take two goats, one would be offered as a blood sacrifice and the other would be kept alive to be the scapegoat for the people. The priest would place both hands on the scapegoat and say a prayer. The prayer was a confession of all the sins committed the previous year. Then the priest would pray that God would place all the blame for their sins on the goat. The goat was then led out into the wilderness and never allowed to return to the camp. In the eyes of the people and in the eyes of God, the goat carried their sins far away.

Isn't it amazing how the Old Testament points to Jesus at every turn? The scapegoat was just a prelude to Christ, who would ultimately become the scapegoat for all humanity. For those that confess their sins and ask for God's forgiveness, Jesus carries their sins far away. The scapegoat that was sent out into the wilderness didn't do anything wrong. He was innocent, but he took the blame for the sins of the people. In this same way, Jesus was completely innocent. But He chose to take the blame for our sins. And when Jesus died, He carried our sin to the grave with Him. And three days later He raised Himself from the dead. Jesus had complete victory over sin and death and He wants you and me to experience the same.

Is Jesus your scapegoat? If He is, your sin debt was paid in full when He died on the cross.

Because He raised Himself from the grave, one day you too will be raised to eternal life.

Scripture Reference for the Day: "The other goat, the scapegoat chosen by lot to be sent away, will be kept alive, standing before the LORD. When it is sent away to Azazel in the wilderness, the people will be purified and made right with the LORD." (Leviticus 16:10)

Day 17

When the Bible talks about the fear of God, it is talking about an all-encompassing respect. I remember as a child, my mom saying to me, "You wait until your father gets home!" I knew when she said that, I was in trouble.

I wasn't afraid of my dad because I knew that he loved me. But I did have a respectful fear of his authority. In other words, I knew he had the power to punish me when I did something wrong.

The Bible teaches that God the Father is all-powerful and all-seeing. He knows every hair on our heads, and he knows every word we are going to say before we say it. Knowing these things should strike some level of fear in the hearts of believers. Even Jesus said that we should fear God. In Luke 12:5 Jesus said, "But I tell you whom you should fear: Fear Him who, after your body has been killed, has authority to throw you into hell; yes, I tell you, fear Him!"

Electricity can help us better understand what godly fear should look like. Electricity is a good thing. Without electricity, we could not refrigerate food, cool our house in the summer, or heat our house in the winter. Nearly every appliance we own, runs on electricity. In the 21rst century, a constant supply of electricity is a necessity for most people.

If God was respected to the extent electricity is respected, we would all be better off. We don't see people going around sticking their fingers in electrical outlets. But we do see people sticking their finger in the face of God all the time. God created electricity and yet most people show more respect for His creation than they do Him. Obviously, we should have a greater fear of God than we do His creation. God is here to help us, but if we do not respect Him, we will eventually hurt ourselves. We have forgotten that God is the most powerful source in the universe!

Lack of faith and understanding is the main reason many Christians do not fear God as they should. If people really knew God, they would be in awe of Him. There are hundreds of scriptures that command us to fear God. And there are hundreds of scriptures that tell us to respect God and His authority.

Every one of us is going to be held accountable for what we did or didn't do in this life. Don't you think it is time to give God the respect He commands? If you do not fear God in this life, you will spend eternity wishing you had.

Scriptural Reference for the Day, "The fear of the LORD is the beginning of wisdom, And the knowledge of the Holy One is understanding." (Proverbs 9:10)

Day 18

Pastor John Harper was just one of many godly people that died the night the *Titanic* sank. He was a Scottish Baptist preacher and well-known evangelist. I read that Pastor Harper preached up to three or four sermons a day. The movie *Titanic* did not come close to portraying the faith that many believers displayed the night the great ship sank.

Pastor Harper led a crusade to make sure that all the women and children were safely on the lifeboats before any of the men. Then he made sure the unsaved men were allowed on the remaining lifeboats before any Christians. He wanted the lost to live so that they might know Jesus before they died. After the ship sank, he continued his crusade. Floating in a lifejacket, he shouted to everyone he saw, "Believe on the Lord Jesus Christ!!"

There was a man swimming in the water nearby, so the Pastor asked him if he knew Jesus. When the man replied that he didn't know Jesus, Pastor Harper was compelled to respond. And he urgently explained his need to accept Jesus Christ as his personal Lord and Savior. John Harper's last words were, "I don't need this, but you do; I am not going down—I am going up!" Then he threw the unsaved man his life jacket.

Four years later that same man showed up at a reunion for the *Titanic* survivors. The man gave this testimony and shared that he had accepted Jesus as His Lord and Savior because of the words and actions of Pastor John Harper.

Since the beginning of time, faith has been the mark of God's servants and it will remain that way until Jesus comes back.

Scripture Reference for the Day: "By faith we understand that the universe was formed at God's command so that what is seen was not made out of what was visible." (Hebrews 11:3)

There is a type of unity that is ordained by God, and there is also a unity that is not of God. It is imperative that we, as believers, know the difference. Either we are united with God or we are not, we cannot have it both ways.

Have you ever wondered why God confused the languages of mankind and why He scattered them to the ends of the earth? The answer might surprise you. The plan to build the tower in Babel revealed that there was strong unity among God's people, but it also revealed their lack of unity with God. To understand this, we need to take a close look at Genesis 11:1–9:

> Now the whole world had one language and a common speech. As people moved eastward, they found a plain in Shinar and settled there. They said to each other, "Come, let's make bricks and bake them thoroughly." They used brick instead of stone, and tar for mortar. Then they said, "Come, let us build ourselves a city, with a tower that reaches to the heavens, so that we may make a name for ourselves; otherwise we will be scattered over the face of the whole earth."
>
> But the LORD came down to see the city and the tower the people were building. The LORD said, "If as one people speaking the same language they have begun to do this, then nothing they plan to do will be impossible for them.

Come, let us go down and confuse their language
so they will not understand each other."

Because of this the people stopped building the city. That is why it was called Babel,
because there the LORD confused the language of
the whole world. From there the LORD scattered
them over the face of the whole earth.

Three times in Genesis, God gave the command to "multiply
and fill the earth." For humanity to manage Earth's resources properly, the entire earth needed to be occupied. However, man failed
to obey God's command. In fact, the command to fill the earth was
ignored for many generations. God knew if mankind lived in one
geographical area, it would not take long for them to run out of the
natural resources needed to survive. So God did something that we
do not see Him do very often. God overruled the free will of man.
And in doing so, He saved humanity from destroying itself.

Scripture Reference for the Day: God blessed them; and God said
to them, "Be fruitful and multiply, and fill the earth, and subdue it;
and rule over the fish of the sea and over the birds of the sky and over
every living thing that moves on the earth." (Genesis 1:28)

Marriage was created by God to be a holy institution. Marriage is the lifelong union between a man and a woman joined together in love. Marriage honors and reflects the character of God. In fact, marriage is so holy that God uses the marriage model in describing the Church's relationship to Jesus.

Today, there are some dangerous misconceptions concerning marriage that need to be addressed. The two issues I want to mention here are same *sex marriage* and *polygamy*. On the issue of multiple wives, some people argue, "The men in the Old Testament had many wives, therefore, having multiple wives was ordained by God." But just because the Bible records something, does not mean that God endorses it! God never condoned homosexuality or polygamy. Remember, the Bible is filled with both history and moral absolutes. To understand the Bible, we must first be able to separate biblical morality from historical facts.

When it comes to God's original design for marriage, there are no gray areas in the Bible. When addressing the issue of same sex marriage, Dr. Alex McFarland said, "We need to share some timeless truths during these truth-less times." And I couldn't agree more. For the first time in America, we are seeing Christians punished for simply refusing to celebrate something that God has called sin. Homosexuality is a behavior that God has condemned. Across America we have seen Christian business owners fined and run out of business for simply refusing to participate in same-sex marriages.

We shouldn't be too surprised by this. Jesus said in John 15, "If the world hates you, you know that it has hated Me before it hated you. A slave is not greater than his master. If they persecuted Me, they will also persecute you."

The good news is that the Kingdom of Heaven is available to every person. It doesn't matter who you are, where you live, how you live, or what you have done. But you must be willing to place your trust in Jesus and believe what the Bible says about sin. You cannot trust Jesus without trusting in His Word, repenting and asking for forgiveness.

There comes a time in the life of every believer when we should understand that personal opinions are not nearly as important as we once thought. Let me be clear, wisdom does not come by the way of human opinion; wisdom comes from the word of God. In fact, any opinion on any issue that contradicts God's Word is an opinion coming from someone who has not yet surrendered to the Lordship of Christ.

Jesus is the one who defined marriage as being a union between one man and one woman. And this same Jesus is the one who created you, and the only one who can save you.

Make no mistake, Jesus had the first word and He will have the last word! In fact, Jesus is the Word. John 1:1 says, "In the beginning was the Word, and the Word was with God, and the Word was God."

Scripture Reference for the Day: "For this reason a man shall leave his father and his mother, and be joined to his wife, and they shall become one flesh." (Genesis 2:24)

Day 21

In 1 Corinthians 13:13, Paul says "And now these three remain: faith, hope and love, but the greatest of these is love." For a long time, I was puzzled by Paul's statement. I didn't think it was possible to have faith without love, or hope without faith. After all, Hebrews 11:6 says, "Without faith it is impossible to please God." And Hebrews 11:1 says, "Faith is the assurance of things hoped for."

But the Bible does tell us that love is greater than faith and hope. I did a search to see how many times the Bible used these words. I discovered that the word *love* is mentioned more than *faith* and *hope* combined. In the NIV translation, the word *love* is used 686 times, while *faith* and *hope* together are mentioned 638 times.

But this still didn't answer my question.

So, why would the apostle Paul tell us that love is greater than faith and hope? Before I share my thoughts on this, I need to give a shout out to a radio program featured on American Family Radio called *Exploring the Word.* One afternoon I turned on the radio and joined a Bible study led by Alex McFarland and Burt Harper. It just so happened that they were talking about this very subject.

Over the years, Alex and Burt have answered many of my Bible questions. If it were not for them, this question would still be unanswered. Here is what I learned concerning 1 Corinthians 13:13.

Two of the most important things that a Christian works on in this life are faith and hope. But in heaven we will no longer need faith and hope because in heaven, faith and hope are a reality.

In heaven we will be face to face with Jesus and faith won't be necessary in order to believe Jesus is who He says He is. As for hope, Ecclesiastes 9:4 says, "Anyone who is among the living has hope."

In heaven all our questions will be answered, all promises fulfilled, and all our doubts removed. We will never again have to trust in the unseen because we will be in the company of Jesus.

When a man asks a woman to marry him, he gives her an engagement ring. That engagement ring is a symbol of the promise concerning their future. It is a symbol of the hope and faith that the couple will one day be united in holy matrimony. When that day comes, and they are married, they will no longer be engaged. The hope and faith they share concerning their future wedding day will have become a reality. The promise made was a promise kept.

The Bible refers to the Church as "the bride of Christ." When Jesus gathers his people to Himself, we will be with Him; we will no longer require faith and hope because all of God's promises will have been fulfilled. This means that we will forever be in the presence of Jesus. Our faith and our hope will have become a reality. Love on the other hand will be with us for all eternity. First John 4:8 says, "God is love." Therefore, in heaven, we will forever be in presence of Love. This explains why Paul said love is the greatest of the three.

Scripture Reference for the Day: "And now these three remain: faith, hope and love, but the greatest of these is love." (1 Corinthians 13:13)

Once upon a time, an eagle's egg fell out of a tree but landed safely in a bush. That bush happened to be on a turkey farm. Before too long, a baby eaglet hatched out of the shell. The first things the little eaglet saw were turkeys. Therefore, the eaglet assumed it too was a baby turkey. Because he thought he was a turkey, he grew up trying to be the best turkey he could be. In fact, he got pretty good at being a turkey because he spent his time hanging around turkeys.

One day the eaglet looked up and saw eagles flying directly over the farm. Something began to stir inside of him and he said, "I wish I could be up there with those eagles." However, when he looked around, he knew that his desire to soar the skies was never going to happen. After all, he was a turkey.

An eagle flying by noticed the eaglet on the ground and it flew down to investigate.

The eagle asked the eaglet, "What are you doing down here?" The eaglet said, "I am down here with my family. I live here. After all, I am a turkey." The eagle looked at the eaglet in disbelief and said, "Someone has been lying to you. You are not a turkey; you are an eagle." The eagle told the eaglet to stretch out his wings. The younger eagle complied. He then had him flap his wings. Before he knew it, the eaglet was flying. He said, "Now follow me." As he was leaving, the turkeys shouted, "Where are you going?" The eaglet responded, "I am going to be what I was created to be!"

The eaglet followed the eagle and flew to places he had never dreamed possible. The eaglet had believed that he was a turkey because he listened to the voices around him that told him he was a turkey. Some of us have been lied to for so long that we have never become what we were created to be. Isaiah 40:31 says, "But those who trust in the LORD will find new strength. They will soar high on wings like eagles." When the eaglet learned the truth, the truth set him free. The same is true for you and me once we surrender to the truth of God's Word.

Scripture Reference for the Day: "And do not be conformed to this world, but be transformed by the renewing of your mind, so that you may prove what the will of God is, that which is good and acceptable and perfect." (Romans 12:2)

Most of us have a spare tire in the trunk of our car. We don't think about it very often; in fact, we forget about it until we need it. But when we have a flat tire and we find ourselves on the side of the road, that's when we remember it and are thankful for it!

Sadly, many of us treat God like a spare tire. Oh, we are glad He is there, but still we just ignore Him and go about our daily lives. Some of us forget all about Him until circumstances arise that we can't resolve on our own. It is only during hard times that we tend to go to God. One of the best ways to demonstrate our love for God is for us to value the importance of His presence in our daily life.

An old man and his granddaughter were walking, working their way through the crowd at the busy carnival. They passed the carnies, games of chance, and dozens of food vendors. But what really caught the little girl's attention was the kiddie rides. She desperately wanted to run and check out all the rides. Ultimately, her desire to roam around and to be entertained got the best of her, and she tried to wiggle her hand free from the grasp of her grandpa. Fortunately, her grandfather wasn't having any of it, and refused to release his grip on her little hand. When she realized that she wasn't going to be able to get away, she began negotiating with her grandfather. She said, "Grandpa, I have a great idea, I will hold your hand, but you don't hold my hand."

Sometimes we try to negotiate with God in a similar way. We don't want God holding us back. We want to run around and to be entertained. So we remove ourselves from His protection and do what is right in our own mind. God will not force His will on us.

It is left up to us to hold God's hand, and much of the time, we fail miserably.

Don't be like those that negotiate with God. Don't say to God, "I will hold your hand, but you don't hold my hand." Don't treat God like you would a spare tire. God loves you and He has great plans for you. Unless you embrace His Lordship, you will never experience the wonderful things He has in store for you.

Scripture Reference for the Day: "For I know the plans I have for you," declares the LORD, "plans to prosper you and not to harm you, plans to give you hope and a future." (Jeremiah 29:11)

Day 24

Think back to your childhood and try to remember when everything was new. Remember how you viewed with amazement the things concerning God's creation? Psalm 104:24 says, "O LORD, how manifold are your works! In wisdom have you made them all; the earth is full of your creatures."

To a child the world is a place of mystery and wonder. It is a place where the innocent discover themselves, and God who created it. I remember as a child the wonder and the sense of awe I felt the first time I noticed that a seed could sprout into a living plant. I also remember how awestruck I was when I first witnessed a caterpillar's miraculous transformation into butterfly. These things fascinated me as a child, and yet as an adult I have grown used to them. And I am not alone.

Most of us no longer find miracles like this as fascinating as we did as children. As we get older, we tend to take God's miracles for granted. In fact, most adults rarely ever think about the miracle of life or the world that God created.

Being a grandfather has opened my eyes to a world once lost. I am once again able to see the world as child. I wish everyone could view the world through the eyes of a child. When I do, my faith in miracles is renewed and my sense of awe concerning God and His creation is magnified. God is doing miracles every day. The question is, are you too busy or too numb to notice?

Scripture Reference for the Day: "Everyone kept feeling a sense of awe; and many wonders and signs were taking place through the apostles." (Acts 2:43)

Day 25

A middle-aged man went to a local barbershop to get a haircut and to have his beard trimmed. As the barber began to work, they began to have a good conversation. They talked about various subjects but when religion was brought up, the barber said, "I don't believe that God exists."

"Why would you say that?' asked the customer.

The barber answered, "Well, you only have to go out in the street to realize that God doesn't exist. If God exists, why are there so many sick people in the world? Why do people suffer? Why is there so much hate in the world? No, if God existed, there would be no suffering, pain or hate! I can't imagine a loving God who would allow any of these things." The customer did not respond because he did not want to start an argument. The barber finished, and the customer left the shop. As he was leaving, he noticed a man with long dirty hair, and an untrimmed beard begging for money. The customer was a strong believer and he knew right away that God had timed this encounter. He turned around and headed back in to barber shop. The barber asked, "Did you forget something?" The customer said, "No, I Just wanted to let you know that barbers do not exist!"

The surprised barber retorted, "How can you say that? You must be crazy! I am standing here, and I am a barber! In fact, I just cut your hair!" The customer explained, "Yes, but barbers don't exist, because if they did, there would be no people with dirty long hair and untrimmed beards, like that man outside."

The barber responded, "Ah, but barbers *do* exist! That's what happens when people do not come to me!"

"You just made my point for me," said the customer. "God does exist, but many people still refuse to come to Him!" He went on to say, "In God's future kingdom, all the pain and suffering along with every evil intention will cease to exist. Even sin itself will be eliminated." Eventually the barber received Jesus as his Lord and Savior. And to this day, he tells this story to the new customers as he cuts their hair.

The reason there is so much pain and suffering is the same reason why we have to experience death. We live in a fallen world for now. But in heaven, we will no longer be burdened by the power of sin. And because of the absence of sin; pain, suffering, and death will also cease to exist. Therefore, let me encourage you to persevere in this life. Remember, our time here on earth is short when compared to eternity.

Scripture Reference for the Day: "For since the creation of the world His invisible attributes, His eternal power and divine nature, have been clearly seen, being understood through what has been made, so that they are without excuse." (Romans 1:20)

Day 26

John 8:36 says, "So if the Son sets you free, you will be free indeed." However, the freedom Jesus is speaking about, doesn't come easy. Most of us must suffer before we are set free. Let me explain it this way. Prior to receiving Christ, we are in bondage to sin. And that sin is the cause of much of our suffering.

Prior to surrendering my life to Christ, being set free from the bondage of sin was by far the most painful experience I had ever known. Having had severe back problems that included surgery I knew something about pain. Though the pain associated with confronting sin is different, it is painful just the same.

Hebrews 4:12 explains it this way, "For the word of God is alive and active. Sharper than any double-edged sword, it penetrates even to dividing soul and spirit, joints and marrow; it judges the thoughts and attitudes of the heart."

People don't want to see themselves as unrighteous, ungodly and self-absorbed. And I have never met anyone who wanted to see himself as a prideful and greedy sinner. But that is what we all are without Christ. God's Word supernaturally causes us to see our self as God sees us. So instead of going to God and asking Him to change us, we alienate the only one who has the power to help us. We know the truth is going to hurt, so we avoid it.

A forest ranger found a bear caught in a trap. The bear was in obvious pain and saw the ranger as a threat. The ranger shot the bear with a tranquilizer dart, so he could get close enough to release the bear's paw from the trap. The bear—being drowsy from the drug—thought the forest ranger was trying to hurt him. Then to make matters worse, the ranger had to push the trap further into the bear's flesh to release the clamp on the trap. This caused the bear even greater pain. The bear didn't understand, that without the pain, he could never be set free.

When God releases us from the snares of deception, like the bear, we mistakenly think that God is hurting us, when in reality He is setting us free. Only in retrospect, can we see that God had our best interests in mind the entire time. James 1:2–4 says, "Consider it all joy, my brethren, when you encounter various trials, knowing that the testing of your faith produces endurance. And let endurance have its perfect result, so that you may be perfect and complete, lacking in nothing." C. S. Lewis said, "The question is not 'Why do the innocent suffer?' but rather 'Why don't we all suffer more?'" C. S. Lewis obviously understood the importance of suffering. I have never met anyone who enjoys suffering. But it is comforting to know that God is drawing us closer to Himself, during the trials and tribulations of life.

Scripture Reference for the Day: "For in Christ Jesus the law of the Spirit of life has set you free from the law of sin and death." (Romans 8:2)

Day 27

The Bible is filled with examples of men and women of courage. These men and women took a stand on the word of God, even in the face of certain death. Jesus never lived as a meek person who was afraid of hurting someone's feelings, and neither did any of his disciples. The biblical interpretation of the word *meekness* is much different than how we interpret the word today. Meekness in the Bible is not passivity: it is strength under control. Second Timothy 1:7 says, "For the spirit that God has given us does not make us timid; instead, his spirit fills us with power, love, and self-control."

Think of a wild horse that has been broken and is now tamed. The horse is still as strong and as powerful as it was when it was wild, but now his power is under the control of its master. In this same way we need to be tamed. Have you reached a point of meekness to where you have given control of your life to God.

Only two people in the Bible were described as meek: Jesus and Moses. Neither of them were weak. They were strong men of conviction.

God's values need to become our values and they need to be preached from every pulpit and proclaimed by every believer. Christians should never blend in with the crowd, but they should stand out in a crowd.

Shadrach, Meshach, and Abednego were three young men determined to worship the only true God. In the face of death, they stood firm, unwilling to kneel before a counterfeit god. The people hated them because of their willingness to stand. Daniel was thrown in the lions' den because he was kneeling before his God three times a day. He knew that a law had been passed, preventing him from worshiping his God, yet he did it anyway, despite the threat against his life. In the cases of Daniel and his friends, Shadrach, Meshach, and Abednego, God supernaturally intervened on their behalf. These men didn't "go along to get along." They followed God even though it was unpopular and dangerous.

Most self-proclaimed Christians are afraid of rocking the boat. Their fear of offending the unrighteous outweighs their fear of God. Daniel was seen kneeling while everyone else was standing. Shadrach, Meshach, and Abednego were seen standing while everyone else was kneeling. All four of these men were more concerned about offending God than they were about offending the people around them. Are you willing to put yourself out there for Jesus? Are you willing to stand out in a crowd and show others what the biblical definition of meekness looks like? Are you ready to allow God's strength to be seen in you?

Scripture Reference for the Day: "Who will rise up for me against the wicked? Who will take a stand for me against evildoers?" (Psalm 94:16)

Day 28

The people had been waiting for this day their entire life. The triumphant entry of the King of Israel was at hand. They joyfully scattered palm branches on the streets in front of Jesus as he rode into Jerusalem on a donkey. People were celebrating and shouting, "Hosanna!" The crowd displayed their immense joy by dancing and singing in the streets.

The donkey Jesus rode had never seen a celebration of this magnitude. This made him feel very good about himself. After all, he was carrying the son of God on his back. In fact, before he left that morning he told his mother, "Of all the donkeys in the world, I have been chosen to carry Jesus." The following day, the donkey walked down the same street again. But this time, no one was celebrating in the streets. No one was shouting "Hosanna!" and no one was scattering palm branches in front of him.

Everything was quiet. He tried retracing his path to rekindle the emotions he had felt the day before. But it wasn't the same. He went home and told his mother, "Yesterday I felt so special, but today there is no one celebrating. There was nobody there to greet me when I walked down the street. I felt so good about myself yesterday, but today everything is as it was before." His mother looked him in the eyes, and said, "Son, without Jesus, you are just a donkey."

In 1 John 4:16 the Bible tells us, "God is love." Without love there is no happiness and no contentment. Those who do not have God in their heart are like the donkey in this story. They retrace their steps. Some even choose to live in the past, in an effort to revisit a happier time.

Unfortunately, these folks will never know true happiness and contentment unless they receive Jesus as their LORD. The good news is, Jesus loves you, He is available, and He wants to come into your heart.

Without Jesus, we are all like the donkey in this story. We search aimlessly for our purpose in life. But the good news is that you are not a donkey. You can take Jesus everywhere you go. But first you must make Him the LORD over your life. And once you do, God will begin to reveal to you the answers you seek.

An unknown author once wrote, "I found the answer right there in my very room. The Fan said, "Be cool." The Roof said: "Aim high." The Window said: "See the world." The Clock said: "Every minute is precious." The Mirror said: "Reflect before you act." The Door said: "Push hard for your goals." And the Carpet said: "All this is futile if you do not kneel down and pray to your heavenly Father."

Scripture Reference for the Day: "The LORD himself goes before you and will be with you; he will never leave you nor forsake you." (Deuteronomy 31:8)

Day 29

When our focus is not on God, Satan is free to misalign our priorities and to fill our minds with deceitful lies. Sometimes Satan's ways can be very subtle. But we can be sure of one thing: Satan's goal is to lead people away from God. He usually uses things that appear entertaining and innocent. Satan has even used personal horoscopes to lead people astray.

If you want to know the future, the only source you should trust is the written word of God. After all, Christians know how the story ends. But despite this fact, many believers still read their horoscope daily. Here lies the danger in this. If by coincidence, one day a horoscope forecast "came true," it is likely that even a Christian would become captivated, or at the very least, they would become curious enough to do it again. This could lead them to look to astrology for advice and guidance, rather than to God. Satan is cunning, and he will use things that society does not consider dangerous to lead us away from God.

Adults are not the only ones being led astray in this way. Children are being desensitized to the dangers of the occult through entertainment. One former witch who is now a Christian says that the *Harry Potter* books are dangerous because millions of young people are learning how to contact demon spirits and are even calling them by name. A common belief among many evangelical Christians is that *Harry Potter* promotes the religion of Wicca. Here is what Paul Hetrick, a spokesman for Focus on the Family, said about the *Harry Potter* series: "There are some powerful and valuable lessons about love and courage and the ultimate victory of good over evil; however, the positive messages are packaged in a medium—witchcraft—that is directly denounced in the Scriptures."

Whatever your thoughts are on this issue, or any spiritual issue for that matter, it is vital that you take it to God. If you go to God with a sincere heart and an open mind, He will give you a greater understanding and you will be able to make wise decisions concerning these things.

But let me say this: God does take witchcraft and sorcery very seriously! God warns us not to play around with the occult. This includes tarot card readers, who claim to know the future or speak with the dead. In 1 Samuel 28, Saul consulted a medium to speak to the Samuel, who had died. And from the spiritual realm, Samuel made it clear that God was displeased with Saul for using sorcery. In fact, Samuel called him an enemy of God. Isaiah 8:19 says, "Someone may say to you, 'Let's ask the mediums and those who consult the spirits of the dead. With their whisperings and mutterings, they will tell us what to do.' But shouldn't people ask God for guidance? Should the living seek guidance from the dead?"

The Bible is clear. The occult is something we should avoid at all costs. It is vital that we take our relationship with God seriously, otherwise we might be caught off guard. We can never be too serious when it comes to things God warns us against.

Scripture Reference for the Day: "When you enter the land the LORD your God is giving you, do not learn to imitate the detestable ways of the nations there. Let no one be found among you who sacrifices their son or daughter in the fire, who practices divination or sorcery, interprets omens, engages in witchcraft, or casts spells, or who is a medium or spiritualist or who consults the dead. Anyone who does these things is detestable to the LORD; because of these same detestable practices the LORD your God will drive out those nations before you." (Deuteronomy 18:9–12)

Day 30

In fourth-century Korea, a man had two sons. The older son rose to become the chief justice and the younger son became an infamous bandit. The older brother loved his younger brother but was unable to persuade him to change his ways. Eventually they arrested the younger son who was brought before his brother. Everyone in the courtroom thought the younger brother would get off with a light punishment because everyone knew that the chief justice loved his brother. But to the astonishment of everyone, the chief justice sentenced his brother to death.

On the day of the execution, the elder brother went to the prison and recommended that his brother swap places with him. The younger brother agreed, thinking that once they realized that the prisoner was the chief justice the execution would not go forward. But he didn't realize the extent of his brother's integrity and the passion he had for justice. The chief justice allowed himself to be executed. Filled with remorse, the younger brother turned himself over to the authorities. Their reply to him was, "No one with that name owes a debt to society; that person's crimes have been paid for, in full."

In the same way, Christ died for our sins. Jesus sacrificed Himself so that all our sins against God the Father would be paid for in full. A true believer trusts Jesus enough to turn away from their sin and give Him ultimate authority over their life. When we accept His forgiveness, we are accepting His Lordship over us. If you have not done so already, ask Jesus to be the Lord over your life today.

Scripture Reference for the Day: "If we confess our sins, He is faithful and just to forgive us our sins, and to cleanse us from all unrighteousness." (1 John 1:9)

Day 31

When my brother in-law John Nick was killed in a work-place accident, everyone who knew him was in shock. John was married to Peggy, my wife's identical twin sister. When I heard the news of John's death, I was immediately compelled to write this letter. When I was done, I asked God if He would make sure that John got my message. If someone would have told me that one day I would write a "Dear John" letter, I would have told them that they were crazy. But that is exactly what I did. I decided to share this letter with you, hoping that you might be encouraged by it:

> *Dear John, I think all of us are still in shock over the news of your death. No one but God could have foreseen this tragic and unpredictable accident. You and I married identical twin sisters and when we visited each other, we never were at a loss for words. You are going to be missed by many people here, especially your family. But you can go to the Lord with the assurance that Peggy and Lucy will have all the support a family can give. I will call and check in on them on a regular basis.*
>
> *When I think about you, what I remember the most was your gift of hospitality. You made sure that your house was always home to whoever was visiting. In addition, your ability to fix things never ceased to amaze me. I never believed in a million*

years anyone could get that old rusty tractor to run, but somehow you did it.

Please know that your death will not be in vain. Through this experience, sons and daughters will have a deeper affection for their fathers and mothers. Husbands and wives will have more appreciation for the time they have left together.

Everyone who knew you will be reminded of just how fleeting life can be. Yes, John, I am certain that God will bring a lot of good out of what seems so sad right now. There is an appointed time for everything, and the time will come when we will meet again."

Your Brother In-law and friend,
Tod

Scripture Reference for the Day: "There is an appointed time for everything. And there is a time for every event under heaven a time to give birth and a time to die." (Ecclesiastes 3:1–2)

Day 32

There was an elderly man who decided to visit a new church. He was disappointed from the moment he entered the doors. The first thing he noticed was the lack of eye contact from the greeter. In the sanctuary prior to the service starting, he saw children running around with no apparent supervision. And he was sure that some of them were chewing gum. Once the service started, he noticed that a man two rows up was sleeping. The music was way too loud, and the sermon went well beyond 12:00. As he left the church he said to himself, "I will never come back to this place again—it's full of sinners and hypocrites."

There was another elderly man visiting a church for the first time. The first thing he noticed when he went through the doors was the sincerity of the people that greeted him. He noticed that this church was filled with people of all ages. He noticed the smiles of little children and their seemingly endless supply of energy. He noticed the attention they received from the elderly. He felt a strong presence of the Lord. The music was great, and the message was powerful. As he left the church, he said to himself. "I cannot wait to come back next Sunday. I can see myself serving at this church."

Would you be surprised to hear that both men attended the same church on the same day? If the truth be told, they both got exactly what they wanted out of their experience. The first man was more interested in his own satisfaction than he was in spiritual things. The second man, on the other hand, was obviously more interested in the things of God than he was in himself.

Remember, when God evaluates His people, He investigates the depths of their hearts. When was the last time you asked God to reveal the areas of your life that are displeasing to Him? This is something that we as believers need to do every day.

Scripture Reference for the Day: "I thank Christ Jesus our Lord, who has given me strength, that he considered me trustworthy, appointing me to his service." (1 Timothy 1:12)

Day 33

Sir William Ramsey (1851–1939) was a very wealthy man. He was an outspoken atheist and he held a PhD in archaeology from Oxford. Ramsey hoped to prove that the Bible was just a book of fiction. But he was certain that at the very least he would find factual inconsistencies and inaccuracies in the Bible through archeological and historical evidence. He started an expedition in the Middle East that lasted twenty-five years with the objective of disproving the book of Acts. He chose Acts because it contained so many detailed descriptions of locations and events. But to his surprise, he discovered hundreds of relics that confirmed the historical accuracy of the book. After spending millions of dollars on his research to prove his theory, he had concluded the opposite—the Bible was accurate down to the smallest detail. He stunned the world when he later declared himself a Christian in one of his books. In his own words, he concluded that it would take more faith to maintain his atheism than to believe that the Bible was true and accurate.

For anyone who doubts the authenticity of the Bible, may I suggest seeking the truth? Anyone honestly seeking to know the facts will ultimately come to the same conclusion Ramsey did so many years ago. The Bible was not written to be a work of science, but science continues to back up the authenticity of the Bible. Scientific principles were in the Bible thousands of years before modern day science proved them true. These facts cannot be explained away by anyone in the atheistic movement.

The disciples knew Jesus before He was crucified, and they knew Him after He was resurrected. Most of them were ultimately martyred for their faith. Many years ago, Earl Williams said to me, "Men will not normally die for something that they know to be a lie; but they will die for what they know to be true." When a person believes in his heart that the Bible is the Word of God, he will be both willing to live for Christ and to die for Him.

Scripture Reference for the Day: "In as much as many have undertaken to compile an account of the things accomplished among us, just as they were handed down to us by those who from the beginning were eyewitnesses and servants of the Word, it seemed fitting for me as well, having investigated everything carefully from the beginning, to write it out for you in consecutive order." (Luke 1:1–4)

Day 34

People are asking, "Why are we experiencing all of these natural disasters?" Progressives are placing the blame on what they call *man-made global warming*. When I investigated this, I discovered that satellite data shows no significant global warming in the past eighteen years. There has always been climate change; however, mankind does not control it. In fact, there is substantial evidence to support that the global warming narrative is nothing more than a hoax and a power grab by those with an agenda for a one-world government. Whatever the case, it is absurd to think that mankind could somehow control the weather. What is even more absurd is the fact that a government has the audacity to force hurtful regulations on American businesses based upon narratives they themselves know to be false.

In our culture, when someone makes a comment or alludes to a natural disaster as a possible judgment from God, they are perceived as lunatics. Personally, I believe that there are storms that God sends as judgment. In fact, throughout the Bible, we see God using the elements He put into place to accomplish His will. But I also believe that there are storms that are just part of a natural response to these elements at work. It is also important to remember that we live in a fallen world. Nature is an important part of this world. But, when sin entered the world through Adam, nature itself was corrupted just like everything else.

One day Jesus will come back, and when He does, order will be reestablished. Even the weather will be under His control. Here is food for thought—consider the time when Jesus calmed the storm. If God sent the storm that frightened the disciples, and it was God who told the storm to be still, *God would be telling God what to do*! Jesus said that a Kingdom divided cannot stand. God is in control, but sometimes He allows nature to do what He designed it to do. Sometimes God intervenes when it is in His will to intervene.

Sometimes God will intercede, and a storm will pass us by based on the prayers of faithful followers. Sometimes God will send judgments by the way of nature when He wants to get our attention. Who are we to question God? Matthew 24:6–8 says, "You will hear of wars and rumors of wars but see to it that you are not alarmed. Such things must happen, but the end is still to come. Nation will rise against nation, and kingdom against kingdom. There will be famines and earthquakes in various places. All these are the beginning of birth pains." Jesus did not tell us to rejoice in this type of destruction, but He does want us to find comfort in the midst of the storm.

Scripture Reference for the Day: "For He causes His sun to rise on the evil and the good and sends rain on the righteous and the unrighteous." (Matthew 5:45)

Day 35

A newly ordained minister visited a certain man's house at the request of the man's family. The man he was visiting believed in God, but like so many others, he feared what he did not understand.

The doctors had told him he was dying and that his time was almost up. He asked the preacher, "Exactly what happens to us in the hour of death?" The inexperienced preacher thought for a moment and then replied, "I'm afraid I can't give you an exact answer to that question." As he was leaving, he desperately wished he could say something comforting. As he reached for the door to leave, he heard scratching and whining on the other side. Suddenly, he remembered that he left his dog in the car with the window partially down to allow for some fresh air. So, the moment he heard the familiar sound of a puppy whining, he knew his dog had somehow squeezed through the small opening in the car window. He figured he came to the door of the sick man's house because it was the last place the puppy had seen him. And as soon as he opened the door, the eager dog leaped into his arms. In an instant, God revealed to him a spiritual truth he had been unable to articulate to the home owner. Turning to the sick man, he said, "Did you see how my dog acted? He's never been in this place before. He had no idea what was inside; yet when I opened the door, he sprang in without fear, because he knew his master was here!"

We may not completely understand everything that awaits us on the other side. But one thing we do know, is this: our Master is there, and that is enough! Are you as excited about seeing your Master face to face, in the same way the puppy was excited about seeing his master? If you're not anticipating heaven to some degree, then you are not ready to meet your Creator.

Scripture Reference for the Day: "Let not your heart be troubled; you believe in God, believe also in Me. In My Father's house are many mansions; if it were not so, I would have told you. I go to prepare a place for you. And if I go and prepare a place for you, I will come again and receive you to Myself." (John 14:1–6)

Day 36

It was during the editing process of this book that I learned of Reverend Billy Graham's death. And I was immediately compelled to write a few words about this incredible man and include them in this devotional. Billy Graham's son Franklin Graham recently said, "My father once said, "Someday you will read or hear that Billy Graham is dead. Don't believe a word of it. I shall be more alive than I am now. I will just have changed my address. I will have gone into the presence of God."

Indeed, Billy Graham has changed addresses, and has gone on to be with the LORD. And without a doubt, he has already heard Jesus say, "Well done my good and faithful servant." Graham died of natural causes on February 21, 2018, at his home in Montreat, North Carolina, at the age of ninety-nine. He was a beloved Christian evangelist and an ordained Southern Baptist minister.

Billy Graham will be remembered for his love of God and for his love for the souls of mankind. His ministry reached to the uttermost parts of the earth and will continue through the Billy Graham Evangelistic Association and the work of his children in ministry. I will continue to pray for and to work with the BGEA to strategically place their *Decision* magazines.

Billy Graham will always be revered as one of the most influential preachers of the twentieth century. My heart aches knowing that this great man of God is no longer with us. No one understood the importance of the Great Commission more than Billy Graham. The world lost—and heaven gained—one of the greatest souls of our time. Other than the Apostle Paul, perhaps no other evangelist has done more for mankind than Billy Graham. And even though I know how much he will be missed, my heart rejoices that he can finally rest from his work.

I thank God for sending Billy Graham into the world and offer my deepest condolences to the entire Graham family.

Scripture Reference for the Day: "Go therefore and make disciples of all the nations, baptizing them in the name of the Father and the Son and the Holy Spirit, teaching them to observe all that I commanded you; and lo, I am with you always, even to the end of the age." (Matthew 28:19, 20)

Day 37

As a child, comic book superheroes fascinated me. At a very young age, Superman became my favorite hero. In the world of DC Comics, Superman is the strongest man in the universe—he is invincible. Well, *almost* invincible.

In the world of Superman, there is also a green, glowing substance called kryptonite that can cause him to become as weak as a little baby. Superman is invincible except for that very important vulnerability.

Outside of the fantasy realm of superheroes and in the real world, super powerful entities reside in the spiritual realm, including evil ones. Satan and his demons are fallen angels who want to destroy the souls of men. And Satan is a powerful enemy to this world, but he is nothing in comparison to Jesus.

Jesus is Satan's kryptonite. In the presence of Jesus, Satan becomes as weak as a little baby. To a non-believer these truths can seem to be nothing more than another fictional comic book. But for those of us who have opened our hearts and have received the message of the cross, the truth is evident. The believer understands that the supernatural spiritual warfare going on behind the scenes is real. For them the question is not, "How can somebody believe these things?" The question is, "How can anyone not believe?"

Today, Jesus is my superhero, and unlike Superman, Jesus is very real. And unlike my superheroes of yesteryear, Jesus truly is invincible.

Scripture Reference for the Day: "Great is our LORD and mighty in power; his understanding has no limit." (Psalms 147:5)

Day 38

I have a deep concern for our nation, but I still believe that the Lord is not finished with America. I am so thankful for those who sacrificed their lives to protect our God-given freedoms and independence. We owe them a great deal of gratitude. However, we must never forget that God is the author of our liberty. Years ago, I attended a church service with my youngest daughter and her family on Memorial Day. That same weekend I was moved to write this poem.

"Hope for America"

Wake up America, and do not fret;
God is not finished with this nation yet.
Join me in this prayer of repentance;
Surrender to God, your unbridled resistance.
"Father, loosen the scales, let them fall from our eyes;
That we might see past the enemy's lies.
This is not about America, being lifted on high;
It's about exalting You, with our eyes to the sky.
This is not about America, standing proud and tall;
It's about our ears hearing You, when you call.
It's not about our emotions, or about how we feel;
It's about working together to accomplish Your will.
Fear not America and praise Jesus, our Rock;
He will never grow weary of defending His flock.

Scripture Reference for the Day: "The Lord is the one who goes ahead of you; He will be with you. He will not fail you or forsake you. Do not fear or be dismayed." (Deuteronomy 31:8)

Day 39

In 1855 Joseph Scriven's mother became ill and was on her death bed. Joseph had experienced a tremendous amount of loss in his early adult life. His first fiancée drowned the night before they were to be united in holy matrimony. In response, Joseph donated all his worldly possessions to the poor. Then he left Ireland and immigrated to Canada.

While he was teaching in Port Hope, Canada, he allowed himself to love again. Eventually, he got engaged for the second time. Just before their wedding, his second bride-to-be became ill and died of pneumonia.

Joseph had loved three women in his life. Two of them died tragically leaving him heartbroken. The only woman left that had captured his heart was his mother. And now she was about to die. He wrote a song to encourage his mother prior to her death. The words are still being sung to this day. Regarding the lyrics, he said, "The Lord and I did it between us." He had lost so much and yet he understood that Jesus was sufficient to see him through it. He knew that a close relationship with Jesus was by far the most important friendship he could ever have. He also knew that his relationship with Jesus was the only relationship that death did not have the power to separate. It was during a time of tremendous heart ache and in the midst of incomprehensible suffering, that Joseph Scriven's wrote the words to the hymn, "What A Friend We Have in Jesus."

What a friend we have in Jesus,
All our sins and griefs to bear!
What a privilege to carry
Everything to God in prayer!
O what peace we often forfeit,
O what needless pain we bear,
All because we do not carry
Everything to God in prayer!

Scripture Reference for the Day: "No longer do I call you slaves, for the slave does not know what his master is doing; but I have called you friends, for all things that I have heard from My Father I have made known to you." (John 15:15)

Day 40

A ten-year-old boy decided to study judo even though he had lost his left arm in a car accident. The boy began lessons with an old Japanese judo master. He liked the challenge, but he couldn't understand why, after three months of training, his sensei had only taught him one move.

One day he gathered the courage to ask, "Sensei, shouldn't I be learning more moves?" "This is the only move you'll ever need to know," the sensei replied. Not quite understanding, but believing in his teacher, the boy kept training.

Several months later, the sensei took the boy to his first tournament. Surprising himself, the boy easily won his first two matches. The third match proved to be more difficult, but after some time, his opponent became impatient and the boy used his one move to win that match also.

Everyone was amazed when he went on to win the tournament. On the way home, the boy asked, "Sensei, how did I win the tournament with only one move?" "You won for two reasons," the sensei said. "First, you've almost mastered one of the most difficult throws in all of judo. And secondly, the only known defense for that move is for your opponent to grab your left arm, and you don't have one."

The boy's biggest weakness had become his greatest strength. When we learn to trust in God to the extent that this ten-year-old boy trusted in his sensei, we will begin to accomplish things that we once thought to be impossible.

Scripture Reference for the Day: "Trust in the LORD with all your heart and lean not on your own understanding; in all your ways acknowledge Him, And He shall direct your paths." (Proverbs 3:5, 6)

Day 41

There has always been controversy and questions concerning the story of Moses and the hardening of Pharaoh's heart. During a question and answer segment on Exploring the Word, Dr. Alex McFarland and Pastor Burt Harper talked about this topic. On this particular radio broadcast, McFarland made this comment, "I don't believe Pharaoh needed much in the way of persuasion to rebel against God." But the question remains, did God take over the Pharaoh's intentions?

Ultimately God was the reason for the Pharaoh's hardened heart. J. Vernon McGee once said, "The same sun that melts the wax, hardens the clay. It is the substance of the object and not the sun that allows wax to melt and clay to harden."

God is not going to suddenly harden you. So what should we say about Pharaoh's heart? Pharaoh already possessed a hardened heart. And remember, God is the only source of good in the universe. So by simply removing Himself from Pharaoh, morality and righteousness were sure to disappear as well. Remember, God did cause the plagues, and it was ultimately the plagues that caused the Pharaoh's heart to become hardened. Therefore, by His actions, God did harden the Pharaoh's heart.

If we learn anything from today's lesson, it is this: when a person rejects God, and continues in their sin for too long, God will eventually turn that person over to their sin. Even evil people have some good in them if God is in the midst. Good cannot exist where God is absent. And God doesn't have to remain where He is not wanted.

God gave us the free will to make our own decisions. Some churches have doctrines which allow their interpretation of predestination to excuse them from any accountability. God does not take over our lives and intentions, nor does He take away any responsibility on our part. Pharaoh's pride and his disregard for human life made it easy for him to experience a hardening of the heart.

You might say that Pharaoh was the cause of his own demise. God's attribute of being omniscient allowed Him to know beforehand any decision that Pharaoh would make. Dr. Alex McFarland said it this way, "I do not believe that the Pharaoh's situation was an exception to God's divine practice of allowing free will. When we are reading the Bible, it is important for us to remember that God's nature and His attributes never change."

Scripture Reference for the Day: "Moses and Aaron performed all these wonders before Pharaoh; yet the LORD hardened Pharaoh's heart, and he did not let the sons of Israel go out of his land." (Exodus 11:10)

Day 42

There was a young man who like so many others, spent his days partying and finding new ways to break the law. He was due to go to court in four weeks for the many crimes he had committed. So he decided to spend what he considered his last few weeks of freedom, partying.

After robbing a liquor store, he went to the lake with some of his buddies. He got drunk and fell out of the boat. At first, he fought to stay afloat. But it didn't take long for him to disappear under the water. Fortunately, an older man in the vicinity saw what had happened. He jumped into the lake and retrieved the lifeless body. Once he got the young man to the shore, he immediately began performing CPR. His efforts were rewarded, and the young man's life was spared.

Four weeks later, the young man was in court wondering what his punishment would be. He had committed so many crimes that both he and his lawyer expected a prison term to be handed down. He was surprised when he realized that the judge was the same man who had saved his life that day at the lake.

After overwhelming evidence was given against the young man, he was found guilty by the jury. To his surprise, the judge sentenced him to the harshest penalty the law would allow. Afterwards, the young man said to the judge, "A month ago you saved my life but now you are sending me to prison. What is up with that?" The judge replied, "A month ago, I was your savior; today, I am your judge!"

Friends, Jesus is coming back and when he does, there will not be any more chances. The Bible teaches that Jesus is coming back to judge humanity. Are you ready for your court date with Jesus? If you are not ready, no amount of money, and no lawyer in the world will be able to help you. Complete and unconditional forgiveness is the only defense that will save a person from their sin. To be forgiven, you must believe that the word of God is true and you must trust Jesus as your personal LORD and savior. Have you turned from your sins and asked Jesus for forgiveness? Have you allowed Jesus to be the Lord over your life? Don't wait until tomorrow—it might be too late. The Bible says "Today is the day of salvation."

Scripture Reference for the Day: "Jesus answered, "I am the way and the truth and the life. No one comes to the Father except through me." (John 14:6)

Day 43

God knew the day and the hour Jesus would be born, and God knew when Jesus would be crucified. God also decided the exact time that Jesus would be raised from the dead. From the very beginning, everything was planned to perfection. And let us not forget, God has also chosen the day and hour of Christ's return.

Barnabas was one of the early Apostles martyred for his faith. Scripture paints a picture of Barnabas as a compassionate and forgiving man. Luke said this of Barnabas, "He was a good man, full of the Holy Spirit and of faith." Luke also said that wherever Barnabas went a great many people were added to the Lord. The Epistles of Barnabas were not included in the Scriptures; therefore, we must not consider them to be divinely inspired in the same way we do passages in the Bible. Many scholars, including my friend and mentor, Dr. Don Davidson, believe that the epistles of Barnabas were probably written around 130 AD and named after him. Only God and Barnabas know whether the epistle is really the words of Barnabas. And only God and Barnabas know whether they were divinely inspired.

However, I feel compelled to share a portion of these writings to encourage whoever is reading this to consider the possibility that their time to get serious about God may be coming to an end. Keep in mind, I am not trying to date the return of Christ. But considering current events I do find these writings very intriguing.

In the Epistle of Barnabas, there is a prophecy that says mankind will have six thousand years of history and then Christ will return and reign for one thousand years:

> "Give heed, children, what this means; He ended in six days. He means this, that in six thousand years the Lord shall bring all things to an end; for the day with Him signified a thousand years; and this He himself bear me witness, saying; Behold, the day of the Lord shall be as a thousand years.
>
> Therefore, children, in six days; that is in six thousand years, everything shall come to an end. And He rested on the seventh day. This He means; when His Son shall come, and shall abolish the time of the Lawless One, and shall judge the ungodly, and shall change the sun and the moon and the stars, then shall He truly rest on the seventh day."

According to the Hebrew calendar, the year 5776 began at sunset on September 13, 2015.

Many Biblical scholars believe that Jesus might return in our lifetime. Matthew 24:36 says, "But about that day or hour no one knows, not even the angels in heaven, nor the Son but only the Father." If that didn't get your attention, perhaps this will. The Irish Saint Malachy prophesied in 1139 AD, there would be 112 popes from his time before the end came. Is it a coincidence that Pope Francis is the one hundred and twelfth pope? Time will tell if we are as close to the end as some of us believe.

I don't claim to know when Jesus is coming. However, I do believe that there is sufficient evidence to support that the day of our Lord's return is drawing near. Jesus gave us many warning signs so that we would be watching and anticipating His arrival. Considering all these things, I can say with assurance, there has never been a better time to seek God.

Scripture Reference for the Day: "He who testifies to these things says, 'Yes, I am coming soon.' Amen. Come, Lord Jesus." (Revelation 22:20)

God's Word addresses the issues that are currently dividing this country. One of these can be found in Deuteronomy 22:5. This verse says, "A woman shall not wear anything that pertains to a man, nor shall a man put on a woman's garment, for all who do so are an abomination to the LORD your God."

For years LGBT* activists, with the support of Hollywood elites and the mainstream media, have been able to advance their agenda by claiming that people are born gay. Under the leadership of former president Obama, the United States government became involved in supporting this ideology. And the LGBT movement has been gaining momentum ever since. We have seen things take place that no one thought possible a decade ago. Millions of people have bought into the LGBT lie that says people are born gay. This dangerous movement ignores medical science, biology, human anatomy, and DNA. Perhaps even more importantly, it ignores thousands of people who have left this life style to pursue a God honoring life style. My heart aches for those who have bought into their lies and are now caught in their web of deceit.

LGBT activists claim that homosexuality has nothing to do with a person's feelings because they were born that way. But when it comes to transgendered people, it is all about their "feelings!" We all know that feelings can change. Unfortunately, the entire ideology behind the LGBT movement is based upon feelings rather than truth. LGBT activists say if a boy feels like a girl on Monday he

---

* *LGBT is shorthand for "lesbian, gay, bisexual and transgender."*

should be able to shower with the girls. But if he feels like a boy on Tuesday, he should be able to shower with the boys.

The double standard here is obvious. They say homosexuals are born that way and can't change. But then they say that transgendered people can change depending on how they feel on any given day. When it comes to LGBT, ideology always trumps reality. And make no mistake about what their real agenda is: a new sexual revolution and the marginalization of God. Therefore, those of us who believe the Bible are in their way. With that in mind, it is important to understand that both homosexuals and transgendered people make up less than 4 percent of our population. The transgendered alone make up less than 0.3 percent of the population.

When it comes to the lefts' push to allow men in women's bathrooms, showers, and changing rooms, transgender people are not my main concern. My main concern is that sexual predators and pedophiles use policies like this as opportunities for sexual gratification. When it comes to sexual predators, dangerous policies such as this one is viewed as an opportunity to exploit and take advantage of women and children. Common sense tells us that the more opportunities we create for pedophiles to be alone with our children the more we are going to see our children abused. How can we in good conscience enable grown men this kind of access to our women and children? We are leaving our loved ones in a state of extreme vulnerability. Privacy is necessary for the security of our women and children. This is obviously creating an unsafe environment. These policies obviously endanger women and children, but they also put transgendered people at risk.

The LGBT agenda is an all-out assault against God and utter rebellion against God's design.

Think for a moment about how far we have moved away from our basic values. Not long ago there were laws that protected young girls from grown men exposing themselves to them. Now bills are being written that could legalize this behavior. Moreover, corporate America is bullying states and threatening to take their businesses out of any state that would refuse to comply and celebrate this intrusion of privacy. Businesses like Target and PayPal are leading the charge to normalize this sinful behavior. The Obama administration had threatened to remove federal funding from any school that refused to allow teenagers in the bathrooms, locker rooms, and showers of their sexual counterparts. I thank God that President Donald Trump made it a priority to put a stop to this all-out assault against biblical morality. Obviously, Christianity is the left's biggest obstacle.

The mainstream media refuses to make this an issue, and when they are compelled to talk about it, they side with the LGBT community, the democratic party, many Hollywood elites and college professors. The recent decision by the Supreme Court to change God's definition of marriage was more of an attack on the Church than it was about same-sex marriage.

My dear friends, we are under assault! What are you going to do? Will you hide in the shadows, or will you speak out against these atrocities? Will you stand on the word of God?

Scripture Reference for the Day: "If my people, who are called by my name, will humble themselves and pray and seek my face and turn from their wicked ways, then I will hear from heaven, and I will forgive their sin and will heal their land." (2 Chronicles 7:14)

Day 45

One afternoon a beautiful swan landed on the bank of a large pond where a crane happened to be pacing about looking for snails. The crane observed the swan for a few minutes and then he asked, "Where did you come from?" "I come from heaven!" replied the swan. "And where is heaven?" asked the crane.

"Heaven is in heaven" said the swan, "Have you never heard of heaven?" And the beautiful bird went on to describe the magnificent eternal place. She told the crane about the streets of gold. She told him about the pearly gates. Then she went on to describe the beautiful walls made of precious stones.

Then she told him about the River of Life, and how the water was as pure as crystal.

The eloquent terms the swan used to describe heaven didn't arouse even the slightest interest in the crane.

When she had finished talking, the crane asked: "Are there any snails there?" "Snails!" repeated the swan; "No, of course not!" The crane continued its search along the slimy banks, and said, "You can have your heaven. I'll stay here with these snails!"

This story contains some deep hidden truths. How many young men have turned their backs on God, in the search of snails? How many young women have deliberately rebelled against God, only to learn too late that they had forfeited a place in heaven? And for what, *snails*? How many men and women have sacrificed their entire families, for the snails of sin?

I say, "One is too many." If you were to miss out on one thing in life, I hope, for your sake it's not salvation.

Heaven is a place of unspeakable beauty. It is a place where only the people of God go. It is the place where believers are constantly in the presence of God for all eternity. It is a place where the curse of sin and all its effects have been removed forever. Acts 14:22 calls this place the Kingdom of God. And the Kingdom is one of beauty. Its splendor is beyond anything our imaginations can come up with. Revelation 21:3 reads, "And I heard a loud voice from the throne, saying, 'Behold, the tabernacle of God is among men, and He will dwell among them, and they shall be His people, and God Himself will be among them.'"

Scripture Reference for the Day: "He will wipe away every tear from their eyes; and there will no longer be any death; there will no longer be any mourning, or crying, or pain; the first things have passed away." (Revelation 21:4)

Exodus 4:11 says, "The LORD said to him, 'Who gave human beings their mouths? Who makes them deaf or mute? Who gives them sight or makes them blind? Is it not I, the LORD?'" This raises the question, "Why would God allow His people to become handicapped, terminally ill, or to be born deaf, mute or blind?" To get the answer to this question, we need to understand that we live in a fallen world. And we must also believe that when it comes to disease and handicaps, that God has a good reason for interceding in the lives of the people He created. Because we live in a fallen, chaotic world, it is much better for us if God controls the chaos. God uses the less fortunate to bring out the best in others. In this world, there will be poverty and there will be disabilities. The handicapped and the less fortunate will be with us until Christ comes back. If no one had it worse than we do, we would have no reason to even think about their suffering. But because someone is always suffering more than us, we can experience compassion and empathy. This world in its current condition has a lot of problems. But can you imagine living in a fallen world where there was no empathy or compassion?

I repeat, we live in a fallen world! And in a fallen world, bad things are going to happen to good people. Perhaps God directs where and when these bad things happen. Then again, the Bible says, "God shows no favoritism." There are some things that are not meant to be understood this side of heaven. What we do know, is that God can bring good from a bad situation. I am just thankful that God chose to stay involved with His creation even after sin entered the world. Disease and suffering are going to exist in a sin infested world.

And I think we forget that life is but a blink of the eye when compared to eternity. Isaiah 64:8 says, "Yet you, LORD, are our Father. We are the clay, you are the potter; we are all the work of your hand." And Romans 9:21 says, "Does not the potter have the right to make out of the same lump of clay some pottery for special purposes and some for common use?"

Trust God enough to give Him the benefit of the doubt, He knows the best way to reach the most people.

A child who has cancer gives someone else a passion to help children with cancer. A blind person causes someone to have compassion for the blind. In heaven things will be perfect.

My point is this, we must never pick and choose the Scriptures that we want to believe. Because when we do, we are designing a God to our own liking. Either the Word of God is true, or it is not. If you choose to design your own god, you are making for yourself a counterfeit god—and a counterfeit god cannot save or answer prayers.

A world without sickness and death can only work in a world without the sin nature. That world is not here yet. But it will come when Jesus returns.

There is good news for God's people. Indeed, God will heal those He afflicted. The suffering and sickness experienced in this world will seem like a bad dream. But even that dream will vanish. The illnesses we experience this side of heaven are nothing in comparison to the eternity of wellness God has planned for His people. Isaiah 30:26 says, "The moon will shine like the sun, and the sunlight will be seven times brighter, like the light of seven full days, when the LORD binds up the bruises of his people and heals the wounds He inflicted."

Scripture Reference for the Day: "You shall not add to the word that I command you, nor take from it, that you may keep the commandments of the LORD your God that I command you." (Deuteronomy 4:2)

Day 47

As a child, I loved watching the *Star Trek* series. Whenever the *Starship Enterprise* was under attack, Captain James T. Kirk would give the order to raise the shields. The shields were like a force field; a thin, invisible and yet impenetrable barrier, which completely encompassed the ship and was able to deflect the weapons used against them by their enemies.

The entire starship and the lives of its five-hundred-plus passengers depended on these shields holding up to, and withstanding attacks from the enemy. Unfortunately, the force field on the *Starship Enterprise* was flawed. These shields could only take so much abuse before they would become weak and no longer offer any protection. In addition, they could not go on the offense while the shields were up. They had to lower their shields before they could fire any weapons. And to make matters worse, the *Enterprise* could not use the transporter while the shields were up. This means they could not bring anyone under the safety of the force field if they were outside its protection prior to the attack.

This starship had technology far beyond the present. Yet even with all the technology that this great vessel of science fiction has, it fails in comparison to our God and the reality of Him as our protector. God offers us a supernatural force field. Sometimes we call it God's umbrella of protection or we might call it His "hedge of protection." Unlike the force fields we see in science fiction movies, God's protective barrier has no limitations. His all-encompassing barrier of protection can withstand anything the enemy throws at it without ever weakening.

While we are under this supernatural shield of protection, we can still be on the offense and in the fight. In 2 Corinthians 10:4, Paul says, "The weapons of our warfare are not carnal, but mighty through God to the pulling down of strongholds." And perhaps the best part is that we can bring others under the force field of God's protection without having to "lower the shields." God's force field goes with us wherever we go.

Scripture Reference for the Day: "Do not rebel against the LORD; and do not fear the people of the land, for they will be our prey. Their protection has been removed from them, and the LORD is with us; do not fear them." (Numbers 14:9)

Christian values are the root of all our American freedoms, and it is these same Christian values that cause people from all over the world to want to live here. They may not want to share in our values, but they do want to live in an environment that was created by these Christian values. Our problems today are more spiritual than they are political. It is this idea of a government without God that put us into the mess we find ourselves in today. We cannot expect the words in the Constitution to fix any of our problems unless we interpret the Constitution with the same spirit in which it was written. And make no mistake, our founding fathers got their insight from the Bible.

I recently read about something Supreme Court Chief Justice Earl Warren wrote in 1954: "I believe the entire Bill of Rights came into being because of the knowledge our forefathers had of the Bible and their belief in it." We are at a tipping point as a nation. We as a people must decide whether we really want government to be our God. I pray that we will have the will to take back what we have lost and put God in His proper place as the leader of this nation.

President Gerald R. Ford said, "A government big enough to give you everything you want is a government big enough to take from you everything you have." Christianity has the greatest influence on western society. With God in mind, the Founding Fathers achieved a balance between church and state. This balance worked in the past because it was consistent with Biblical thinking.

The University of Houston did a ten-year study. They researched over fifteen thousand documents, finding that 34 percent of the quotations used by the Founders came from the Bible. I am dumbfounded as to why people would seek to undermine a system of government that has worked for over two hundred years, especially when they have benefited from the very freedoms they are determined to take away.

Scripture Reference for the Day: "Furthermore, you shall select out of all the people able men who fear God, men of truth, those who hate dishonest gain; and you shall place these over them as leaders of thousands, of hundreds, of fifties and of tens." (Exodus 18:21)

Day 49

A people-pleaser is what many Christians believe is an acceptable example of someone who is loving and caring. Some justify this behavior by claiming that they are the peacemakers Jesus spoke about in Matthew. It is vital that we as believers understand this statement: a peacemaker and a people-pleaser are not the same thing! The problem with people-pleasing is that acceptance usually trumps morality. A peacemaker's motives are pure, while a people-pleaser is looking to be accepted. The peacemaker understands that sometimes the truth hurts. The people-pleaser is willing to forego the truth. A peacemaker fears God and does not want to offend Him. The people-pleaser fears people and therefore, they are more afraid of offending people than they are of offending God. The best interest of others is the driving force behind the peace maker. But the pleaser just wants to fit in or to gain a sense of self-worth.

People-pleasers believe that righteousness means being nice. Niceness and righteousness are completely unrelated ideas. But in an effort to be politically correct, we have made these two words interchangeable. While the Bible doesn't say to be nice, it does command righteousness. Niceness adapts and changes depending on the situation and the people you are talking to. Niceness refuses to offend people. In other words, truth is set aside in order that a person's feelings might be spared. There is no biblical account that supports this behavior. Righteousness, on the other hand, is cemented in the scriptures.

In Galatians 1:10, the Apostle Paul used the Greek word *aresko* when talking about people-pleasers. *Aresko* means to strive to accommodate oneself to the opinions and desires of another. Every believer's goal should be to praise and seek God's approval—not the approval of man.

Scripture Reference for the Day: "For am I now seeking the favor of men, or of God? Or am I striving to please men? If I were still trying to please men, I would not be a bond-servant of Christ." (Galatians 1:10)

Day 50

I used to worry that I was going to die while I was doing something that I knew I shouldn't be doing. I remember on numerous occasions begging God not to allow me to die drunk. I had a true death wish when I was walking in disobedience. For this reason, I would continuously ask God to let me die sober.

Tommy Cash, Johnny Cash's younger brother, once said, "I don't know if there is any particular thing that I want to accomplish, other than I want to die sober." My words echoed Tommy's for many years. But after I surrendered to the Lord, dying sober was no longer enough for me. I was compelled to discover God's will for my life. I was convinced that God's plan for me consisted of more than just sobriety, and I am even more convinced of this today. I hope my words help someone else who is struggling. My prayer is that this book will help others who are desperately seeking to overcome a lifestyle of habitual sin.

It was only when I became desperate for God that he took charge of my life. For most of us, deliverance doesn't take place overnight. My prayer was usually two-fold. I would ask God not to give up on me, and then I would ask God not to allow me to give up on myself. If you feel as if I am talking about you, please take some advice from a person who has been in your shoes. Keep seeking God in both the good times and the bad. If you are sincere, if you recognize your sin, and if you recognize God's holiness, He will honor your persistence. And when you are ready, He will deliver you from the spiritual chains holding you captive. Remember, God looks at the heart and He knows you better than you know yourself. And once you come to the end of yourself, God will do a great work in you.

God delivers those who surrender to Him. Learning to surrender is a process. For many years I thought all God wanted from me was a commitment to do my best. But God wanted more than a commitment. I wasn't delivered from the bondage of habitual sin until I realized that my occasional commitments to God were insufficient. I was set free when I surrendered and placed myself under His authority. If God will do this for a man like me, I have no doubt that He will do it for you.

Scripture Reference for the Day: "Take delight in the LORD, and he will give you the desires of your heart." (Psalms 37:4)

Day 51

I have had many conversations with God, where I poured out all my heart, mind, and soul to Him. I recall one time when I was weeping uncontrollably. And as I continued to cry out to God, He spoke to my heart. It was so meaningful to me that I was compelled to write down the experience. This is how that conversation went.

I said, "Who am I Lord, that You would shed Your blood and die for me? What did You see in me that no one else, including myself, could see? I am a flawed person, I am lacking in humility, and I am not worthy that You would even consider me. Some days I am unlovable, and at other times I am selfish. Why do You love me so? Why do You still call me to serve in the ministry when You know all these things about me.

I am prideful, and I am judgmental. I am critical of others. And to make matters worse, sometimes I am aware of my sin.

I am inconsistent in my worship, I am inconsistent as a witness, and sometimes I allow my feelings to control my attitude. Why do You continue to put up with me? You know all my darkest secrets, nothing is hidden from your sight, and yet You still see value in me. I am unworthy, yet You give me worth. I am both self-centered and self-absorbed, especially when my focus is not on You. But you forgive me repeatedly. I have let you down so many times: why do You bother with me?"

This is what I perceived to be God's response to me: "All these things you say are true, but you have been blessed with My unconditional love. You are forgiven of all your trespasses. For you have been washed in the blood of My son, Jesus. Your sins will never be counted against you. You are Mine, and no one can pluck you from My hand. And because of the love I have for you, I was willing to pay the ultimate cost to redeem you. Remember, I created You in My own image. Now then, walk in My ways and I will bestow blessings upon you beyond your wildest imagination."

My response to God went something like this, "Now I understand, Lord. Help me to see myself as You do. Help me to see myself as the righteousness of Christ. For when I see myself as You do, I know I am blessed.

However, I do ask that you will never let me forget where I came from, so I can share my testimony with others. The reason I exist—the reason I am—is because You are the Great I Am. Thank You, Lord! Thank You for loving me. Help me to address the areas in my life that you would have me to change. In Jesus' name I pray, Amen."

Since then I have had many similar encounters with God.

If we are completely honest, we would have to acknowledge that we all have room for improvement. Today, my life is no longer about who I am; it is about the fact that God is the Great I Am! I admit, I am far from perfect. However, I do start each day with the intention of making my heavenly Father proud of me. My goal is that someone reading this will be motivated to do likewise.

Scripture Reference for the Day: "God said to Moses, 'I AM WHO I AM'; and He said, 'Thus you shall say to the sons of Israel, "'I AM has sent me to you.'" (Exodus 3:14)

Day 52

A young woman asked a local pastor to come over to her house and pray with her father who was expected to die soon.

When the pastor arrived, he found the man lying in bed with his head propped up on two pillows and an empty chair beside his bed. The pastor assumed that the old fellow was aware that he was coming over. "I guess you were expecting me," he said.

A little confused, the old man said, "No, who are you?"

The pastor replied, "I'm serving as the associate pastor at the church around the corner. When I saw the empty chair, I figured you were expecting me."

"Oh yeah, the chair, sit down and I will tell you about that chair." whispered the old man. "I've never told anyone this, not even my daughter. But all of my life I have never known how to pray. For years I never made any attempt at prayer." He continued, "One day about four years ago my best friend said to me, 'Joe, prayer is just a simple matter of having a conversation with Jesus.' He told me to sit down with an empty chair in front of me, and in faith see Jesus in that chair. He suggested that I speak to Jesus and listen to Him in the same way you're doing with me right now."

Then the old man said, "So I tried it and I've liked it so much that I do it a couple of hours every day. I try to be careful though. If my daughter saw me talking to an empty chair, she'd think I lost my mind."

The pastor was moved by the man's story and encouraged the old man to continue doing what he was doing. They prayed together, and afterward the pastor returned to the church. A few days later, the daughter called to tell the pastor that her daddy had died. "Did he go peacefully?" he asked. "Yes, before I left the house around 2:00 p.m., he called me over to his bedside and kissed me on the cheek and told me to be careful and that he would be just fine. When I got back from the store an hour later, he wasn't breathing. But there was something strange about the way I found him. Apparently, just before daddy died, he leaned over and rested his head on that chair he always kept by his bed. I found him with his head lying on the cushion of that chair."

Tears formed in the minister's eyes as he recalled the conversation he had with her dad. To this day, he believes like I do, that the old man died with his head resting in the lap of Jesus Christ.

His dying action spoke louder than any words, because he displayed a level of faith that we should all strive to achieve. It also speaks of Christ's availability and His great love for you and me.

Scripture Reference for the Day: "Therefore I say to you, all things for which you pray and ask, believe that you have received them, and they will be granted you." (Mark 11:24)

Day 53

Recently I was working on a sermon about the necessity of being "born again," when I felt moved to write this little poem. I love it when God does the unexpected.

JESUS IS WILLING AND ABLE TO SAVE, ALL OF CREATION THIS SIDE OF THE GRAVE!

JESUS IS WILLING TO REMOVE ALL YOUR SHAME, AND HE ACCOMPLISHES THIS BY TAKING THE BLAME!

JESUS IS WILLING TO TEACH AND REFORM, THAT YOU AND I MIGHT BE REBORN!

JESUS IS WILLING TO REDEEM THE LOST, AND FOR THIS, HE PAID THE ULTIMATE COST!

JESUS IS WILLING TO ESTABLISH FOR YOU, A LIFE WITH PURPOSE, A LIFE ANEW!

JESUS IS ABLE TO WASH AWAY SIN, ARE YOU WILLING TO BE BORN AGAIN?

THE QUESTION IS NOT, "CAN CHRIST DO THIS FOR MAN?" THE QUESTION IS THIS, "DO YOU, BELIEVE THAT HE CAN?"

Scripture References for the Day:

1. Jesus replied, "Very truly I tell you, no one can see the kingdom of God unless they are born again." (John 3:3)
2. "You should not be surprised at my saying, 'You must be born again." (John 3:7)
3. "For you have been born again, not of perishable seed, but of imperishable, through the living and enduring word of God." (1 Peter 1:23)

Day 54

My wife and I were babysitting the grandchildren while doing our weekly shopping at Wal-Mart when this experience happened- Isaac,who was twenty months old at the time, was sitting in my cart while Abigail, his younger sister was sitting in Grandma's cart. I had placed a six-pack of Mountain Dew next to Isaac, and the next thing I knew, he was trying to pull one of the twenty-ounce bottles loose from the plastic rings.

I looked at Isaac and smiled, saying, "You know we have to pay for this before we can drink it." What happened next caught me completely off guard. Isaac folded his little hands together, then bowed his head and began to pray. He had apparently mistaken the word *pay* for the word *pray*.

I couldn't understand everything he was saying, just the names of those he was praying for. And although this was humorous, I immediately knew that there were a few things that God wanted to reveal to me through this experience.

I was reminded of Matthew 18:3 were it says, "Truly I say to you, unless you are converted and become like children, you will not enter the kingdom of heaven." My grandson's example reminded me of how we should be ready to pray in any given situation. We should be willing to pray even over the little things. Many times, we find ourselves going to God in prayer only when we are overwhelmed or suffering.

God has revealed so much to me through my grandchildren. But God has also revealed many things to me through the elderly residents at the assisted living facilities where I hold church services.

I have gained wisdom from both the young and the old. The older folks have experienced things that the next generation will have to read about in books. But I have also gained understanding from the child-like faith of children. Through my grandchildren, I have learned to see the world in new and exciting ways. In conclusion, both the young and the old have so much to give, and through them, we have so very much to gain.

Scripture Reference for the Day: "Is not wisdom found among the aged? Does not long life bring understanding?" (Job 12:12)

Day 55

My daughter Sarah was probably twelve or thirteen years old when her Grandma Barney decided to take her to the theatre to see a movie. When the movie started, so did the inappropriate language.

True to her nature, Grandma Barney immediately took my daughter by the hand and walked out of the theatre. It was this experience that made me realize just how blessed my children are to have the support of godly women. They have had wonderful women of integrity and courage serve as their role models. Integrity and courage is exactly what Grandma Barney displayed that day at the theatre. That was years ago, but my feelings about Grandma Barney have never changed. I am honored to know and love this wonderful woman.

My daughters have been blessed with many wonderful women as role models. They have known the unconditional love of Grandma Salts—my mother—and they have seen what integrity looks like up close from their own mother. They also grew up knowing a great-grandmother who taught Sunday school for over fifty years. They called her Great-Grandmother Oakes. To me, the title *Great-Grandmother* is a testimony to the life of this godly woman. She was great because her humbleness and humility would never allow her to think herself great. I have never met, and I probably never will meet another great-grandmother grander than her. She was truly an oak: just as her last name implied, she was strong and unmovable. The examples set by all these women are rare. of them have made this world a better place.

Scripture Reference for the Day: "I am reminded of your sincere faith, which first lived in your grandmother Lois and in your mother Eunice and, I am persuaded, now lives in you also." (2 Timothy 1:5)

Day 56

Scripture compliments Scripture regardless of where it is found. But perhaps the most amazing thing I have discovered over the years is that Jesus can easily be seen throughout the entire Bible. In fact, all the books of the Bible point directly to Christ.

Jesus said in John 5:39, "You study the Scriptures diligently because you think that in them you have eternal life. These are the very Scriptures that testify about me." In this passage, Jesus confirmed that the Old Testament scriptures were about Him. During his recorded ministry Jesus quoted at least twenty-four different Old Testament verses.

2 Timothy 3:16 tells us that, "All Scripture is inspired by God." Throughout these ancient writings, we read about the promise of a coming Messiah. And in the New Testament we see these promises fulfilled. Max Lucado said, "The Bible is a story of two gardens: Eden and Gethsemane. In the first, Adam took a fall. In the second, Jesus took a stand." The people under the old covenant looked forward to the coming Christ, while we look back on the same Christ, who has already come. Therefore, both the Old and the New Testament are relevant to our daily lives. In fact, the two covenants merged on the day in which Jesus was crucified.

But first it is important for us to understand that hundreds of years before Jesus was nailed to the cross, it was prophesized that He would die in this way. But here is the most amazing part about this prophecy, death by crucifixion was unknown at the time it was written. In fact, it would be nearly seven hundred years later before the Romans invented crucifixion.

What I am about to share with you next helped me to better understand our Heavenly Father's role in making our relationship with Him possible.

In Exodus 26:33 a command to hang the veil was given, "You shall hang up the veil under the clasps and shall bring the ark of the testimony there within the veil; and the veil shall serve for you as a partition between the holy place and the holy of holies." Hebrews 9:7 says, "But only the high priest entered the inner room, and that only once a year, and never without blood, which he offered for himself and for the sins the people had committed in ignorance."

Tradition tells us that the high priest of Israel would enter the Holy of Holies in the tabernacle or temple with a scarlet rope tied to his foot and with bells around his waist. Another priest in the Holy Place tended the other end of this rope.

For if the high priest's sins were not atoned for properly, he would die in the presence of, "The glory of God—that filled the Holy of Holies." Since nobody else could enter that part of the temple without also dying, the priests needed a way to retrieve the body of the high priest, if necessary. That was the purpose of the rope—to pull the body out. The bells were a sign that the priest was still alive. This serves as a powerful reminder of God's holiness and how we should praise Jesus for the direct access to God's throne that He provides! The veil represented the separation between man and God. Matthew 27:51 says, "And behold, the veil of the temple was torn in two from top to bottom; and the earth shook, and the rocks were split." Keep in mind, the temple veil was a curtain that was about sixty feet in height, thirty feet in width, and four inches thick. When I was a kid, I saw a strongman tear a phone book in half that was about two inches thick. This veil was made with multiple layers of compressed curtain. Due to the thickness of the veil, it would have been impossible for someone to physically tear it.

When the veil was ripped, it opened a new pathway for the relationship between man and his God. The veil was ripped from the top down indicating that our Heavenly Father is the one who tore the veil, thereby opening access to Himself. The tearing of the veil was our heavenly Fathers recognition, and acceptance of the blood sacrifice made by Jesus Christ on the cross. It is the most important event in the history of the world because it changed God's throne from a throne of judgment, to a throne of grace for all believers.

Scripture Reference for the Day: "Do not think that I came to abolish the Law or the Prophets; I did not come to abolish them but to fulfill them. "For truly I say to you, until heaven and earth pass away, not the smallest letter or stroke shall pass from the Law until all is accomplished." (Matthew 5:17, 18)

Day 57

When I turned twenty-one years old I felt like had the freedom to do whatever I wanted to do. And like many other young adults, everything I wanted to do contradicted the word of God. There is a reason why sin is so enticing. If we are honest we would have to admit that sin can feel good and be fun. But speaking from experience I can tell you, this kind of fun is short-lived.

Sooner or later, ungodly activity results in unwanted consequences. For those who die without knowing Jesus, these consequences are eternal.

Please consider the importance of what I am about to tell you: *the freedom to sin will not set you free—it will enslave you.*

When you are under bondage to the sin nature, you do not have the freedom to do what is right in the eyes of God. You are enslaved to sin. But freedom in Christ is the freedom to say no to sin. This freedom gives you the ability to choose not to sin by declaring Christ's victory over sin.

Before the internet and compact discs, people used to listen to cassette tapes. My favorite song was on one side, but there was always a flipside. The same is true of righteousness. God's side is the side of righteousness; anything else is the flipside, or the side of unrighteousness. Don't allow yourself to be misled: we choose sides every day of our life. A person can't be spiritually free unless he has the truth, and that truth can only be found in God's Word. The Bible tells us that Jesus is the Word. Jesus said of Himself, "I am the Way, the Truth and the life."

We can live for God or we can remain in our sin. Either way we have a choice to make. If we choose to live life God's way, the Holy Spirit will help us, and we will be set free from our sin. If we choose to remain in our sin, we will become captive to it.

How many of you remember something called the Emancipation Proclamation? This was a very important piece of history. When Abraham Lincoln signed the Emancipation Proclamation into law, all the slaves in America were freed. Hundreds of thousands of slaves were released from their bondage. Sadly, many of the freed slaves were scared because they knew no other way of life. And because of their fear of the unknown they chose to stay and live under the authority of their old masters.

In a similar way, when we accept Jesus as our Lord and Savior, we are set free. And we are no longer in bondage to the sin nature. But unfortunately, just like many of the slaves of yesterday, some of us choose to go back into spiritual captivity by returning to the only life we knew.

I believe, the signing of the Emancipation Proclamation was the most important day in America's history. But the day I surrendered my life over to my Creator was, by far, the most important day of my life.

Scriptural reference (Galatians 5:1): "It is for freedom that Christ has set us free. Stand firm, then, and do not let yourselves be burdened again by a yoke of slavery."

Most of us have either worn braces or know somebody who has. Personally, I have never had braces, but I have heard that they are a constant hassle for the person wearing them. I have been told that wearing braces can be uncomfortable and sometimes painful. My youngest daughter Rebekah had to endure braces as a teenager.

When a person's teeth are crooked, braces are used to straighten them. Constant pressure and tension are needed to successfully straighten what was once crooked. This process can be uncomfortable and even painful. In most cases braces are tightened multiple times before the patient's teeth are straightened out. But when the braces are removed, the results speak for themselves. In a similar way God wants to "straighten us out." And just like it was for the person wearing braces, going through this process is not easy. We must go through some uncomfortable and even painful experiences in order to be straightened out—the Christian life can be hard to endure. But with God's help, all things are possible.

Early in my ministry, pride was an issue for me. I couldn't see it at the time, but in retrospect it is easy to see. There was a time when I actually thought that God needed me. Oh, I think my intentions were good, but obviously my motives were not pure. I was wrong in my assessment of myself and I needed to be humbled in a significant way. Through a series of painful events God began revealing to me my true nature and gave me a desire to change. As I grew in Christ, I began to realize that life was not all about me. God never needed me! It was I who needed God the entire time.

God is going to accomplish what He is going to accomplish with or without me. And I knew if I wanted to be used by God, I had to be willing to embrace God's "spiritual braces." God gave me the fortitude to accept the pain as part of the sanctification process. God will do the same for you. And it doesn't stop there: God often wants us to be braces in the lives of others. Remember 2 Timothy 4:2 says, "Preach the word; be prepared in season and out of season; correct, rebuke and encourage with great patience and careful instruction."

Scripture Reference for the Day: "If either of them falls down, one can help the other up. But pity anyone who falls and has no one to help them up." (Ecclesiastes 4:10)

Day 59

For five years the young man saved his money. He was a hard worker, but he found it difficult to make ends meet. He wanted nothing more than to go on a cruise to the Bahamas. Finally, he had the funds necessary to purchase the ticket. But after doing so, he realized that he had not saved enough money to pay for food on the trip. So he took a jar of peanut butter and a loaf of bread with him.

When the day finally arrived, he was so excited. But soon he discovered that the cruise was not all he expected it to be. While everyone else was enjoying the extravagant buffets, he was alone in his small cabin eating peanut butter sandwiches. After three days of this, he felt he had to say something. He stopped one of the ship's employees and he asked, "Sir, what do I have to do to get one of those meals I see everyone else enjoying?"

The employee looked at the man and asked him, "Do you not have a ticket?"

"Yes, I have a ticket," replied the man. "I spent all the money I had just to buy this ticket." The employee explained that the meals and entertainment were included in the price of the ticket and that he was free to enjoy all of it.

Many Christians live out their lives like the man on the cruise ship. They view their salvation as a ticket to heaven and nothing else. Jesus Christ is sufficient to fill all our needs in this life, as well as our needs in the next. We miss out on so much when we do not receive everything that God has to offer. God's gift to us is more than just the gift of the hereafter; it is a gift for the here and now.

Scripture Reference for the Day: "I have come that they may have life, and that they may have it more abundantly." (John 10:10)

Day 60

God used over forty human authors on three different continents to write the Bible. It was written over a span of 1,500 years and yet there is no evidence of any historical errors. No other book on the entire planet even comes close to these amazing attributes. This is because the Bible was authored by the creator of the universe. Divine inspiration can be found in every chapter of every book. No prophesies or Scriptures found in this holy book came from a writer's own interpretation. This makes the Bible both unique and infallible. The unity of the theme of the Bible cannot be explained away. These men who wrote the Bible lived in different places and in different eras. In most cases they were complete strangers to one another. And yet, in all sixty-six books of the Bible we find perfect harmony in the message the Bible conveys. The Bible has been burned and it has been banned, mocked and ridiculed. In addition, it is currently outlawed in 55 nations. The Bible has overcome more adversity than any other written book. The Bible has not only survived, it has supernaturally thrived. It has been the top-selling book in the world for three hundred years now. So why has the Bible received such utter contempt from mankind?

The reason is simple: The Bible is offensive because it convicts people of their guilt and confronts them with their sin. The saddest part of all this is that the opposition to the word of God usually comes from those who haven't read it. Therefore, there is a strong push to remove Christianity as we know it from American culture.

The Bible has overcome many obstacles and the obstacles seem to keep coming. The latest act of rebellion against God was the redefinition of marriage to include people of the same sex. To God, marriage is a holy institution. In fact, the Bible refers to the Church as the bride of Christ.

Nonetheless, on June 26, 2015, God's Word was overruled by the Supreme Court. Same-sex marriage has been forced on all fifty states through judicial activism, overruling over 40 million voters who voted to protect God's definition of marriage.

Obviously, we have reached a point where mankind has the audacity to think they can overrule God. But let me assure you, God will have the final word! Abortion was forced on America in the same way. In 2016, before leaving office, President Obama tried to force schools to allow boys and girls to share the bathrooms and locker rooms with students of the opposite sex. In addition, he threatened to take away federal funding from any school that did not comply with the mandate. In February 2017, President Trump's administration rescinded the Obama rule concerning students with gender dysphoria. The consequences of rebelling against God are taking a toll on America. Since 1973, when abortion was legalized, nearly sixty million babies have been killed in the womb.

What the majority wants seems to make little difference to those on the political left. America embarked down a very dangerous path when we kicked God of our public schools. Evangelist Tim Todd said, "The very year we removed the Bible from school, 1963, America became number one in violent crimes, illegal drugs, the divorce rate, illiteracy and teenage pregnancy. This can be accurately traced back to the very year the Bible was removed from school. In addition, teen crime has been on the incline ever since the Ten Commandments were stricken from schools." How long do you think God will put up with Americas outright rebellion?

Scripture Reference for the Day: "If anyone causes one of these little ones—those who believe in me—to stumble, it would be better for them if a large millstone were hung around their neck and they were thrown into the sea." (Mark 9:42)

Day 61

An elder Indian Chief was talking to the young braves about the struggle within. He said, "The life of a man is never easy. It is like there are two dogs constantly fighting inside of us. There is a good dog who wants to do the right thing, and there is a bad dog who is bent on doing evil. Sometimes the good dog is stronger and wins the battle. But sometimes the evil dog wins."

A young brave desperate to understand asked, "Who will win in the end?" The wise Chief answered, "The dog that you feed the most will win in the end."

When we spend time in God's word, we grow spiritually and get to know God better. If we stay the course, we eventually learn to recognize God's voice, and we are able to discern good from evil. But remember, the wisdom of God is only revealed to those who seek it. It is by His design, that godly wisdom makes no sense to those who are unwilling to seek it.

First Corinthians 1:18 says, "For the message of the cross is foolishness to those who are perishing, but to us who are being saved it is the power of God." The word of God is truth; it is spiritual food and it is much more important than regular food. If we want to do right by God, it is vital that we know where He stands on the issues. Feeding on the Holy Word produces a biblical perspective that leads us to do what is right in the eyes of God. It takes time and effort to meditate on the Word and to digest it. But when you do, it becomes a part of you. And when it becomes part of you, the good dog wins.

Scripture Reference for the Day: "I gave you milk, not solid food, for you were not yet ready for it. Indeed, you are still not ready." (2 Corinthians 3:2)

Day 62

A snowflake cannot exist on earth unless the temperature in the air and on the ground is as cold as it is. That makes the snowflake one of the most delicate things in all of God's creation. Not only is the snowflake fragile, it is also very interesting, and there is much we can learn from it. The snowflake's individuality is what caught my attention. Did you know that no two snowflakes are exactly alike? The same is true for humans. When observed under a microscope, both your fingerprints and your DNA are uniquely different than everyone else's. God's creativity and His imagination in creation never ceases to amaze me. As I stated previously, the snowflake is a fragile and delicate thing. But consider for a moment what snowflakes can do when they stick together. When pure white snow covers the ground, or it paints a mountain top, it is a beautiful thing to behold. But when it is out of control, it can be dangerous and even deadly.

I remember as a child when the National Guard was called to Goodland, Kansas. This was due to a blizzard, the proportions of which I have never encountered since. Many of us who lived there were snowed in for four days without electricity.

Just like the snowflake, when we stick together, we can either be a beautiful thing to behold or we can become dangerous and deadly. It depends on whether we are united over the word of God or if we are united over something that runs contrary to God's word.

Are you united with God on the things that are really important?

The moral issues we are facing today are the result of mankind uniting against God to normalize sin. As Christians, everything we say and do should reflect the values given to us in the Scriptures.

We should consider it an honor to stand on God's word despite any foreseeable negative circumstances that might arise from doing so. Remember, when we are united with each other, and at the same time united with God, we become an unbeatable force for good.

Scripture Reference for the Day: "Come now, and let us reason together," Says the LORD, "Though your sins are like scarlet, they shall be as white as snow; Though they are red like crimson, they shall be as wool." (Isaiah 1:18)

Day 63

Since sin can sneak in and influence anyone, it is vital that every believer be aware of the civil war that is occurring in their mind. We make the decision either to please God or please ourselves every day. Ephesians 4:24 says, "Put on the new man, which in the likeness of God has been created in righteousness and holiness of the truth." Notice that it doesn't say that God will put on the new man for us. We can't do this without God, but we do have responsibilities that require action on our part. Therefore, it is a cooperative effort between man and God.

It is this combined effort that cleanses our hearts and minds, resulting in a new life; a life of purpose and obedience to God. Because it is a combined effort we refer to it as a relationship. In a way, our relationship with God can be likened to a vacuum. A vacuum cleaner through its own strength can do nothing. It cannot get rid of the unwanted filth without being plugged into a power source. Even then, the vacuum cleaner is useless until it is turned on.

We do not have the ability to clean up our own lives, the power to do this comes from the Holy Spirit. But without our effort, God will not empower us. But even more importantly, without God there is no power for us to plug into.

Are you ready to clean up your life? Are you looking for purpose in life? God is ready to help you in these areas. Do not put this off another day. Plug into the most powerful source in the universe today. Plug into the Creator of the universe. You will be astonished and amazed as you witness the transforming power of almighty God.

Scripture Reference for the Day: "I can do all things through Him who strengthens me." (Philippians 4:13)

Day 64

Matthew Henry was a Christian minister and English commentator of the Bible. He was born in October 18, 1662, and he died on June 22, 1714. He wrote commentaries on all sixty-six books of the Bible. His commentaries are still being used by scholars today. I share in their appreciation for his unique insight into the scriptures, and sometimes I use his commentaries in my own studies.

In addition to his commentaries, Matthew Henry is remembered for his wisdom and his unquestionable faith. But what I appreciate the most about Matthew Henry's life was his willingness to be thankful despite his circumstances. His life was an example of what true thanksgiving looks like.

One evening while taking a walk, Matthew Henry was brutally attacked and robbed. And it was only by the grace of God that he was able to escape with his life. The thieves took everything of value that he had. Later that same evening he wrote in his journal these words: "I am thankful that during these years I have never been robbed before. And even though they took my money, I am thankful that they did not take my life. And although they took all I had, it was not much. Finally, I am grateful that it was I who was robbed, not I who did the robbing." Because Matthew Henry understood the true meaning of thanksgiving, he was able to find multiple reasons for being thankful despite the vicious attack he experienced. We can all learn from his example.

A pessimist says, "My cup is half empty." An optimist says, "My cup is half full." A thankful person says, "My cup runneth over!"

Remember, Thanksgiving is not just a holiday we celebrate once a year—true thanksgiving is a lifestyle.

Scripture Reference for the Day: "Enter his gates with thanksgiving and his courts with praise; give thanks to him and praise his name. For the LORD is good and his love endures forever; his faithfulness continues through all generations." (Psalms 100:4, 5)

Day 65

The intelligent young man knew in his heart that he was ready. This was the day he was scheduled to preach his first sermon. He was confident that his message would be remembered as one of the greatest first sermons ever presented at his home church. Unfortunately, he was so sure of himself that he forgot his need for God. He walked up to the pulpit, tall and confident. He was certain that the people would be impressed by his communication skills. He was so sure of himself, he didn't even take his notes with him when it was time for him to speak. A retired preacher had been watching closely when the young man made his way toward the pulpit. The seasoned minister wasn't sure if what he was picking up on was a young man's pride, or a simple case of extreme confidence. Whatever it was, the Lord was using it to get his attention. His instincts were confirmed when he realized that the young man was experiencing a memory lapse. The young man stood there for what seemed to him to be an eternity. His mind had gone completely blank. The only thing left for him to do was to walk down the stairs and sit in the front row. He was embarrassed and humiliated. It was only by the grace of God that the retired pastor recognized the young man's dilemma and stood up to preach in his place.

After the service the retired pastor explained to the young man the importance of humility. He said, "Young man, if you would've gone up those stairs the same way you came down, you would've come down those stairs the way you went up."

Scripture Reference for the Day: "But he gives us more grace. That is why Scripture says: "God opposes the proud but shows favor to the humble." (James 4:6)

Day 66

John Newton was an anti-slavery preacher and an author. But perhaps more importantly, he wrote one of the most beloved songs of all time, "Amazing Grace." There has never been any doubt that this timeless hymn was divinely inspired. Most every believer knows the words, "I once was lost, but now I'm found... Was blind, but now I see." John Newton chose to live a life of humility. The last words before he died were, "My memory is nearly gone but I remember two things: I am a great sinner, but I have a great Savior!"

When I hear the lyrics "Was blind, but now I see," I also think about another believer by the name of Joan Brock. Joan is a teacher who lost her sight from a rare eye disease at the age of thirty-two. Ironically, she worked at a school for blind children. Five years after the loss of her sight, she tragically lost her husband to cancer. She was left to raise her young daughter as a blind, single parent. But Joan refused to let her visual impairment define her.

In 2003, Joan's life story was portrayed in the Lifetime Television Network movie, *More Than Meets the Eye: The Joan Brock Story*. Joan attributes her successes to her faith in God.

Nowadays, she schedules speaking engagements to share her story. The irony of the blind leading the blind is not what lead me to write about her. But what really caught my attention about Joan Brock was an answer she gave on a radio interview. She was asked, "Considering everything you have been through, 'Have you ever asked God, "Why me?"' In her answer, she made it clear that she could never bring herself to ask God that question. Though she is blind, she obviously sees life more clearly than most. My wife Debby has ALS, and like Joan, she refuses to see herself as a victim. After hearing Joan's reply, and seeing first hand, how my wife handles adversity, I was reminded of the many times that I had asked God, "Why me?" I immediately asked God to forgive me, for all the times I had played the victim. Today I am learning to live victoriously. I thank God for people like John Newton and Joan Brock. But I thank God for my wife most of all. Her favorite song is, "It is Well with My Soul." And it is obvious to everyone that knows her, that no matter what happens to her in this life, it will be well with her soul.

Scripture Reference for the Day: "He replied, "Whether he is a sinner or not, I don't know. One thing I do know. I was blind but now I see!" (John 9:25)

Day 67

In 2011, an atheist named Mr. Greene demanded that Henderson County remove a nativity scene from the Athens, Texas courthouse lawn. The Freedom from Religion Foundation was more than happy to support his effort and to sue Henderson County.

On December 17, 2011, I attended a Christian rally in Athens, Texas, in support of their keeping of the nativity scene. Nearly five thousand concerned citizens from several small east Texas towns came to show their support. And from there, a message was sent to the entire country. This rally wasn't just about a nativity scene, it was so much more.

I learned that there are thousands of Americans who are willing to stand against the liberal media and the repression of Christian values. More and more people are becoming aware of the relentless push of a narrative designed to make people believe that America has never been a Christian nation.

This was never about decorations: it was about the unrelenting continuous attack on religious liberty. I am proud to say; a message was sent from this little town. It was sent to anyone desiring to take away our God-given freedoms. The message is this, "We will not roll over; we will stand with one voice to preserve the Judeo-Christian values that America was founded upon." Though many believers are still silent on the issues, I believe we are still the majority. Despite what you hear in the media, it is high time we make our voices heard. One of the speakers at the rally said, "Yes, God has blessed America. It is time now for America to bless God."

It is time to lock arms with our brothers and sisters in Christ and take this country back to a former time when "In God We Trust" really meant something. But for this to happen, the Church must be willing to take a stand.

Four months after I attended the event in Athens, something in the paper caught my attention. Mr. Greene, who instigated the law suit over the nativity scene, had suddenly decided to drop the lawsuit.

He called a news conference and told reporters he had learned he was going blind. He said that he was going to have to quit his job as a taxicab driver and that he did not have any health insurance. Mr. Greene implied that fighting a legal battle was the last thing on his mind. He was much more concerned about his failing eye sight than he was the nativity scene.

But that's not the end of this story. The last thing Mr. Greene expected was God's people to come to his aid. But that is exactly what happened. He didn't have enough money to pay the rent and to buy groceries when the medical bills started coming in. But to his surprise, churches in the surrounding area began taking donations to help him. The same people that Mr. Greene had sought to persecute were the very people who came to his aid. I read that the first check given to Mr. Greene was for $400 and the money was still coming in. Mr. Greene responded in a way that I did not expect: "My wife and I never experienced Christians acting like this before."

In fact, he was so moved by the generosity and love of the people, that he said that he would like to contribute to Henderson County with some of the money he had received. Mr. Greene said, "I have decided to show my appreciation to the Christian community for all their help, and I am going to buy a star for the top of the nativity scene."

As far as I know, Mr. Greene has yet to accept Jesus as his Lord and Savior. We pray the time will come when he does. What he has experienced will be hard for him to ignore, because what he experienced is the love of Jesus.

Scripture Reference for the Day: "Moreover, I will give you a new heart and put a new spirit within you; and I will remove the heart of stone from your flesh and give you a heart of flesh." (Ezekiel 36:26)

Day 68

Saint Jerome was one of the most important scholars of the early Christian Church. He is credited for translating the Greek manuscripts into Latin and putting the Bible in the language of the people. One night while living in Bethlehem, where Jesus was born, Jerome had a dream in which Jesus visited him.

This dream was so real to him that it influenced the rest of life. In the dream, Jerome collected all the money he had and gave it as an offering to Jesus. Jesus said to Jerome, "I don't want your money." Then Jerome rounded up all his possessions and tried to give them to Jesus. Jesus said, "I don't want your possessions."

Jerome turned to Jesus with tears in his eyes, and asked, "What then, can I give you Lord?" To this, Jesus replied. "Jerome, Jerome, you don't understand. You see, I didn't come for your money or your belongings, I came only for your sins."

Jesus is not asking you for your money or your possessions. Jesus asks that you exchange your sins for His Blessings. How could anyone turn down such a selfless request? But the truth is, many of us hold on to our sin anyway. When I first heard this story, I was brought to tears. Jerome's dream not only pointed out the selflessness of Jesus, it revealed to me the hidden value that I had placed on material things. You see, while I was I listening to this story, like Jerome I was thinking of different items that I could give Jesus. Repenting from my sins and placing them at the foot of the cross never even entered my mind. And that broke my heart. For the first time in my life I understood how my sinful trash could be considered a treasure to Jesus. This is our way of showing Jesus that we love Him. Are you willing to turn away from sin and turn to Jesus? Will you give your sin to Jesus today? Jesus loves you so much. And all He asks in return is that you love Him back. Is that too much to ask from someone who died for you, to offer you eternal life in Heaven?

Scripture Reference for the Day: "He himself bore our sins in His body on the tree!" (1 Peter 2:24)

Day 69

A boy asked his father, "Dad, if three frogs were sitting on a limb that hung over a pond, and one frog decided to jump off into the pond, how many frogs would be left on the limb?"

The dad quickly answered, "Two."

"No." The son replied. "There are three frogs and one decides to jump; how many are left?" The dad said, "Oh, I get it, if one decides to jump, the others would jump too. So there are none left."

The boy said, "No, dad, the answer is three. I said the frog *decided* to jump, not that he did jump."

Many times, we as Christians decide to take a leap of faith, yet we never even get out of the starting gate. We must ask ourselves, am I ready to take that leap of faith? Maybe God has placed it on your heart to learn to witness or join a ministry that shares your passion in a particular area. Maybe God has been leading you to start a new ministry. Or perhaps God wants you to deal with a personal issue such as an addiction or an immoral behavior that you have been living with.

When God has placed something on the heart of a born-again believer, He will keep bringing it back up until that person complies with His will. However, if that same person ignores God too long, there is a real danger of becoming hardened to the point that they can no longer hear or understand God's prompting.

We are the temple of the Holy Spirit and thereby live jointly with God. Therefore, we know what it is that we should be doing. And by the same token, we know what activities need to be eliminated from our life. For this reason, I urge you, my brothers and sisters, do not put off until tomorrow what God has called you to do today. There is no better time to take that leap of faith then right now. You will be glad you did.

Scripture Reference for the Day: "Do you not know that your bodies are temples of the Holy Spirit, who is in you, whom you have received from God? For you are not your own." (1 Corinthians 6:19)

Day 70

God has revealed Himself and demonstrated His involvement in my life many times.

All these occurrences seemed to come during my greatest times of need. They came when I or a loved one was experiencing a physical or spiritual crisis.

The one thing that I can point to that always seems to be a prerequisite to God's intervention has been my willingness to cry out to Him. Even before I knew Jesus as my savior, I cried out to God.

God's intervention always seemed to happen when I was desperate and after I had cried out to Him.

Our approach to God can change with our circumstances, but the one thing that never changes is God's faithfulness to those who cry out to Him.

> Crying out to God displays a sense of urgency that brings about a response from God. For me, crying out to God has always been an emotional heart-led plea, consisting of real tears.

Whether there are tears or no tears shed at all, crying out to God is always accompanied by a broken heart.

God always looks at the heart, therefore, our words to God need to come from our heart. 1 Samuel 16:7 says, "People look at the outward appearance, but the Lord looks at the heart."

Crying out to God is basically bearing our soul to God. It demands that we empty ourselves, by pouring every fiber of our being in to our prayers.

Crying out to God testifies to the fact that we are subject to His mercy. It admits to God that we are powerless, and He is all powerful.

In 2 Corinthians 12:9 Paul wrote, "My grace is sufficient for you, for my power is made perfect in weakness. Therefore, I will boast all the more gladly about my weaknesses, so that Christ's power may rest on me."

When you experience what it means to come to the end of yourself, you will experience a closeness to God unlike anything you have experienced before. And when this happens, God will respond. God will respond in His way and in His timing, but He will respond.

Scripture Reference for the Day: "He fulfills the desires of those who fear him; he hears their cry and saves them." (Psalm 145:19)

Day 71

Jesus loves you. In fact, Jesus loves you so much that He died for you. And all He asks in return is that you would trust him enough to let Him reign as the Lord over your life. In Luke 24:6–7, Jesus said, "the Son of Man must be delivered up into the hands of sinful men, and be crucified, and the third day rise again."

And this is exactly what happened. The only stipulation to becoming a child of God is that we meet Jesus at the cross. It is at the cross where I found Jesus and it is at the cross where you will find Him. My granddaughter Abigail will sometimes stretch out her little arms and say to me, "Grandpa, I love you this much, I love you all the way to heaven and back." One evening she stretched out her little arms like she had done so many times before. And just like the previous times, she said, "Grandpa, "I love you this much, I love you all the way to heaven and back."

But this time I pictured Jesus on the cross. His arms were outstretched, His hands were nailed to that cross. And I could hear Him saying, "I love you this much, I love you all the way to heaven and back." And I knew right away that He meant it literally—because that is exactly what he did. And all Jesus asks in return, is that we would love him back. Is that so much to ask for? Is that too much to ask of the people He died for? I would hope not!

Let's show Jesus how much we love Him by trusting Him with our lives. Most of us already trust Him with the most valuable thing we have: our souls. So why don't we trust Him enough to allow Him to be the Lord over every area of our life?

Let Jesus be the Lord over your mouth, the Lord over your actions, and the Lord over your mind. After all, Jesus did say, in John 14:15, "If you love Me, you will keep My commandments."

Do you take the word of God seriously? Do you trust that the Bible God gave us is true and accurate? Trusting in God this way is how we demonstrate our love for Him. Our obedience to the Word tells God that we believe Him. Let me be blunt: anyone proclaiming to be a Christian who does not believe in the authority of the Scripture is calling God a liar. Jesus summed up what it means to love God in the garden of Gethsemane, when He said, "Not my will, but Your will be done."

Scripture Reference for the Day: "All Scripture is God-breathed and is useful for teaching, rebuking, correcting and training in righteousness." (2 Timothy 3:16–17)

Day 72

The attempt to normalize sinful behavior is evident every time we turn on our television sets. Contemporary television and social-media desensitizes its viewers to indecency and inappropriate material. We are seeing this in movies, online videos, sitcoms, video games, and advertising. When it comes to the advertisers, it is all about the almighty dollar. Most commercials that we see every day contain some kind of sexual innuendo or materialistic propaganda. Nearly every commercial will try to make us believe that we cannot be truly happy, healthy or beautiful unless we use a certain product. The power of marketing is more influential and effective than ever in getting a product recognized and ultimately purchased by the public.

Unfortunately, the little white lies that we hear from the advertisers and media influencers have a negative effect on the people and the culture we live in. For this reason, I have decided to write my own commercial. This commercial will speak the whole truth and nothing but the truth. My commercial will outline a plan designed to change lives for the better. It will guarantee everlasting joy to anyone who voluntarily chooses to participate. It will sound something like this:

> Are you "sick and tired" of being sick and tired? Are you fed up with doing the same old things and getting the same old results? Do you feel like you have been beaten down and held back? It does not have to be this way. Did you know that Jesus was beaten so that you could be unbeatable?

God is in the business of changing lives. If you want a new life, God accepts trade-ins. There is no charge to you: Jesus paid in full for your trade-in, over two thousand years ago. Please don't go another minute without receiving this free gift!

This is a limited time offer. In fact, this offer will expire when you expire. No one knows how long their life will last, so contact Jesus on His toll-free, prayer heart-line today.

This offer comes with a personal guarantee from the Creator of both Heaven and Earth. You will not be put on hold; your call to God will be personal and direct. Best of all, just one application of the Holy Spirit will last for all eternity with an infinite guarantee!

Jesus is operating the prayer station and He is awaiting your call. This is truly the opportunity of a lifetime. Get down on your knees today and call on Jesus!"

Scripture Reference for the Day: "For the wages of sin is death, but the free gift of God is eternal life in Christ Jesus our Lord." (Romans 6:23)

Day 73

When we pray from the heart, either our circumstances change, or we will. If God does not change your circumstances, He will help you to get through them. Wisdom is always a good thing to pray for, and there is no such thing as too much wisdom.

I recently converted a joke I heard into a sermon illustration by simply adding elements of faith, prayer and wisdom to the story line. I hope you get as much out of it as I did.

A little puppy that was lost in the woods when he noticed out of the corner of his eye a huge lion walking in his direction. Not knowing what to do, he began to pray silently to God. He asked God to give him the wisdom he needed considering the situation that he was in. As the lion drew near God spoke to the puppy's heart, and just like that, he knew what he had to do to survive.

The puppy grabbed a bone that happened to be near him and he began to chew on it. Then with his loudest voice he could muster, he growled, "That was the best darn lion I ever ate!" Well, the lion had never seen a critter like this before and he decided it would be best not to mess with it. He did an about face and left the way he came.

A monkey in a nearby tree had been watching the entire time. The monkey thought if he told the lion how this puppy had made a fool of him, the lion would become his friend and protector. And that is exactly what he did. When he told the lion that the puppy was a fraud, the lion was furious. He said, "I am having a puppy for dinner!" So the lion, with the monkey sitting on his shoulders, went in search of the puppy.

Once again, the puppy saw them coming before they saw him. And just like before, he prayed silently to God. And just like before, the little puppy knew what he had to do.

When the lion got within hearing distance, the little puppy kicked up as much dirt as he could with his hind legs. Then he started to pace back and forth. And with a loud voice he yelled, "Where is that darn monkey, I sent him out over an hour ago to fetch me another lion!!"

The little puppy could have prayed differently but he made the decision to pray for wisdom.

King Solomon prayed for wisdom after his father David passed away. God liked what Solomon prayed for so much that He not only answered it, He added blessings to it. God found Solomon's heart to be pure. There was nothing selfish about his request; he simply prayed for wisdom. We would be wise to do the same.

Scripture Reference for the Day: "If any of you lacks wisdom, you should ask God, who gives generously to all without finding fault, and it will be given to you." (James 1:5)

Day 74

The world says that relapses are just mistakes that addicts make. This lie has destroyed many families. If I had not learned to call drunkenness *sin*, I would still be drinking today!

It wasn't a mistake when I went to buy a bottle of vodka—it was rebellion against God! And when I began to see my lifestyle for what it was, I did not like what I saw. This motivated me to fight against the sin nature. But under my own power I failed as often as I succeeded. So I began to look for excuses. Let me be clear, excusing sinful behavior is itself sinful behavior.

Listen to me: drunkenness is a sin! Alcoholism is not a disease; it is a behavior! You can live the rest of your life as a victim, or you can live the rest of your life as a victor. It all depends on your worldview. I choose to believe in a biblical worldview. And in a biblical worldview people do not make excuses for their sin.

What we call alcoholism, God calls drunkenness. The disease theory concerning addiction didn't exist until 1987. It was forced on society to help with the finances in treating people with addictions. Although the intentions may have been good, it greatly minimized any involvement of the Church. Responsibility concerning biblically-based moral issues were once again removed from God's people and placed on the state. While attending classes for the college course *Pharmacology of Addiction,* I remember being told by the professor that if I wanted to pursue a career in drug addiction counseling, I needed to embrace the disease-theory concerning addiction.

The professor went on to say, "If the disease factor were to be taken out of the equation there would no longer be a career path in this field."

Paul said in 1 Corinthians 6:9–11, "Do not be deceived: neither fornicators, nor idolaters, nor adulterers, nor effeminate, nor homosexuals, nor thieves, nor the covetous, nor drunkards, nor revilers, nor swindlers, will inherit the kingdom of God. Such *were* some of you; but you were washed, but you were sanctified, but you were justified in the name of the Lord Jesus Christ and in the Spirit of our God."

Here Paul was saying that they were *formerly* these things, meaning that they are no longer defined by them. Paul made it clear that we are without excuse. Any believer who says, "My problem is hereditary, or I was born this way," is deceiving themselves and contradicting God's word.

By the grace of God, I came to the point where I was able to see myself as having victory in Christ. This was quite a contrast to all those years during which I saw myself as a victim. When the deceiver realizes that you are "in it to win it," he will eventually decide to spend his efforts on someone less dedicated to God.

Scripture Reference for the Day: "But thank God! He gives us victory over sin and death through our Lord Jesus Christ." (1 Corinthians 15:57)

Day 75

We seem to always want God to respond to our prayer requests according to what we want. In addition, we usually want Him to act quickly. And when God doesn't answer right away, we decide to take matters into our own hands.

In 2 Peter 3:9 it says, "The Lord is not slow in keeping his promise, as some understand slowness." However, when we notice time slipping away, we tend to get more and more impatient. It is at this point that we run the risk of interfering with God's intended plans.

In Genesis 16 and 17, Abraham and Sarah received a wonderful promise from the Lord. God told Abraham that he would become the father of many nations. God also told him concerning Sarah, "I will bless her and give you a son from her! Yes, I will bless her richly, and she will become the mother of many nations." For Sarah, giving birth to a son that would carry on his father's name was the most important thing she could do.

Sarah waited on the Lord for many years. But eventually, she made the decision to take matters into her own hands by having a son through a surrogate mother. This was a normal way of overcoming childlessness in those days. But as we will see, going along with the culture does not make it right, especially when God has promised that He would provide.

When Hagar—Sarah's surrogate—slept with Abraham, she conceived and gave birth to a son named Ishmael. But eventually God did keep His promise to Sarah and Abraham. When Sarah was ninety years old and Abraham was one hundred, Isaac was conceived.

However, getting ahead of God always has its consequences. God made two separate nations out of the boys. On one side, we have the descendants of Esau and their allies, the descendants of Ishmael. Ishmael became the father of the Arab people. In 613 AD Muhammad, a descendant of Ishmael, proclaimed himself to be a prophet. Muslim followers of Muhammad have been responsible for Islamic terrorism all around the world.

On the other side, we have the descendants of Isaac. Isaac's son, Jacob, became the father of the Israelites when God changed his name to Israel. This is the bloodline from which Jesus came. Today, the nation of Israel is Americas closest ally.

War between Islam and Israel has been a blood bath to this day. Throughout history, more people have been killed in the name of Islam, than all other people groups combined. Mike Conrad, in an Article in *American Thinker*, rightly said, "Islam is the greatest killing machine in the history of mankind, bar none." Mr. Conrad looked in depth at this and concluded that nearly 250 million people have been killed in the name of Islam. He went on to say, "Even Hitler admired Islam as a fighting religion. He stood in awe of Islam, whose butchery even he did not surpass." Remember, Jesus was Jewish. For this reason, the supernatural hatred for the Jews has continued to grow, and the shedding of blood is a daily occurrence. Sadly, all this began because two of God's chosen people decided to "help God out" rather than to wait upon His timing. Abraham's and Sarah's decision not to wait on the LORD, nearly 4,000 years ago, has dramatically affected the world, and it will continue to do so until Jesus returns.

Scripture Reference for the Day: "I would have lost heart, unless I had believed that I would see the goodness of the LORD in the land of the living. Wait on the LORD; be of good courage, And He shall strengthen your heart; Wait, I say, on the LORD!" (Psalms 27:13, 14)

Day 76

I usually begin my prayer time expecting to have an undistracted quality time with God; however, it is not uncommon for my mind to wander off-course, chasing rabbits that hold no significant value. When I discovered that I was not the only person who struggled with a wandering mind that zoned out from time to time, I wrote this little poem.

"Prayers in the Twilight Zone"

> I was humbly in prayer with God, My boss;
> When suddenly sidetracked, I got lost.
> It was hot, and I was tired;
> I was thinking to myself, "Could I get fired?"
> I stopped a prophet as he passed by;
> And found myself asking, "Where am I?"
> He said, "Son, you're not alone;
> Your lack of focus has put you in a twilight zone."
> "Don't let your mind wander, when you talk to God;
> Stay alert in your prayers from now on, Tod!"

Scripture Reference for the Day: "Pray in the Spirit on all occasions with all kinds of prayers and requests; be *alert* and always keep on praying for all the saints." (Ephesians 6:18)

Loving someone enough to tell them the truth about sin is an act of compassion, not an act of judgment. Still many believers would argue otherwise.

The Scripture that is most often used to support the "Do not judge others" philosophy is, Matthew 17:1. Here Jesus said, "Judge not, lest you be judged." Another popular scripture that divides believers on this topic, is found in John 8:7 where it says, "He that is without sin, let him cast the first stone."

However, when we read these verses in context, Jesus is not warning against godly judgement, but against hypocritical and self-righteous judgement. Romans 2:3 says, "So when you, a mere human being, pass judgment on them and yet do the same things, do you think you will escape God's judgment?" These verses are a warning against hypocrisy and a call to repentance. The intent was never to silence the truth. Christians are called by God to judge between good and evil.

Hebrews 5:14 says, "But solid food is for the mature, who by constant use have trained themselves to distinguish good from evil." We must be discerning of anyone who claims to be Christian, but by their actions reject biblical teaching.

Galatians 6:1 says, "Brothers, if someone is caught in a sin, you who are spiritual should restore him gently." We should have compassion for those caught up in sin, but that compassion needs to include the truth.

If you had a cure for cancer or AIDS, you would share it. If someone was getting ready to jump off a roof top, you would try to stop them. As Christians, we have within us the truth that leads to eternal life. The question we should be asking is, "How can I in good conscience, as a follower of Christ, keep these things to myself?"

When believers rebuke other believers for simply speaking truth, they unknowingly place a higher priority on the *feelings* of the lost, than they do the *eternal souls* of the lost. And without realizing it, they take in their hand the very gavel of judgment that they accuse their brothers of wielding. John 7:24 makes this point very clear. Jesus said, "Do not judge according to appearance, but judge with righteous judgment!"

Scripture Reference for the Day: "Better is open rebuke than hidden love." (Proverbs 27:5)

Day 78

Continuous or habitual sin can eventually harden a person's heart. The danger in this, is that a lost person could be deceived into believing he or she is saved, when in fact, they are not. Our salvation becomes a reality when the knowledge of the Gospel makes its way from our head to our heart. I will never forget the time my friend, Dex Crosby, placed one hand on his head and the other hand on his heart and said, "The longest foot in the world, is from the head to the heart." Saved people trapped in habitual sin will begin to look for ways to justify their sin. And believe me, I am preaching to myself when I discuss this topic. Years ago, I would watch *The Jerry Springer Show*, because seeing people living in despicable ungodly lifestyles caused me to feel better about my sins. The truth is, if we are not careful, we will rate our sin by comparing ourselves to those who we believe are worse than we are.

Eventually we might even dismiss some sins as mere mistakes. We must never declare something to be moral that God has already declared immoral. I have heard the excuse that we live in modern times and some sins no longer apply. I have also heard people say, "If Jesus didn't address it, then it doesn't apply to us today."

Let me point out the foolishness of such statements.

Whenever we read the words *Book of the Law* or *the Law* in the Scriptures, it is referring to the Bible itself. Remember, Jesus had the first five books of the Bible when He walked the earth.

In Matthew 5 ("The Sermon on the Mount") Jesus said, "Do not think that I have come to abolish the Law or the Prophets; I have not come to abolish them but to fulfill them. For truly I tell you, until heaven and earth disappear, not the smallest letter, not the least stroke of a pen, will by any means disappear from the Law until everything is accomplished."

We must never forget that Jesus is the Word of God, therefore, all our *Holy Scriptures* came from Him. The first verse in the book of John says, "In the beginning was the Word, and the Word was with God, and the Word was God." And Second Timothy 3:16 says, "All Scripture is God-breathed and is useful for teaching, rebuking, correcting and training in righteousness."

The truth is, when Christians continue in their sin, they distance themselves from God. The further they move away from God, the less likely they are to hear Him. In Hebrews 3, we are warned about the danger of sin's deceitfulness and how it can harden out hearts. Fortunately, God desires to restore all those who have gone astray. In fact, His desire to restore us is far greater than our desire to be restored. He is willing to go to great extremes to get a person's attention. But ultimately, we make the decision whether we are going to walk in obedience with God.

Do you write off your sins? Do you try to minimize your sins or blame somebody else for them? Today would be a good day to start taking personal responsibility for your sin. When you acknowledge your sin before God and sincerely ask for forgiveness, Jesus will forgive you. There is nothing quite like experiencing a restored innocence of one's self.

Scripture Reference for the Day: "If we confess our sins, He is faithful and righteous to forgive us our sins and to cleanse us from all unrighteousness." (1 John 1:9)

Little Caleb spent an entire weekend building himself a little toy sailboat. When he was finished he wrote his name on the boat with a permanent marker. He was very pleased with what he had made.

He took his new creation down to a nearby stream to see if it would float. He was so happy when he saw this boat float on top of the water. But suddenly and without warning, a strong gust of wind came and the little boat went sailing down the stream. Caleb chased after his boat, but in a matter of minutes it was out of sight.

Caleb was very sad. Caleb continuously searched for his boat, but he never found it. One day while in the local toy store, he noticed a little sail boat on display that looked just like his. When he looked a little closer, he saw that his name was written on the boat. He told the store manager that the boat on display was his. He even showed him his name on the boat, but the manager did not believe him. He said, "If you want the boat, you will have to pay for it; the price is one dollar."

Caleb ran home as fast as his little legs would carry him. When he got there, he took a hammer and broke open his piggy bank. He counted all the change he had saved over the winter. Caleb was so excited when he realized that he had the exact amount that he needed to purchase his boat.

He ran back to the toy store and gave the money to the store manager. As Caleb walked out of the store with his little boat held tightly in his arms, he said, "You are twice mine: first I made you, and then I bought you."

This story is a great example of what our heavenly Father has done for us. God created us. Genesis 1:27 says, "God created mankind in his own image." But because of our sin, we are separated from God. And just like Caleb's little boat, we take the path of least resistance. We go whichever way the wind takes us.

Here is the good news; God seeks us out, even when we should be the ones doing the seeking. Jesus paid the price required to cover our sins. Romans 5:8 says, "But God demonstrates His own love toward us, in that while we were yet sinners, Christ died for us."

God is speaking to the heart of somebody who is reading this message. If that person is you, God wants you to know that you are twice His. First, He made you and then He paid a great price to buy you back. He paid for you with everything He had—His life! He wants you to know that He did this because He loves you.

God's greatest desire is to have a personal relationship with you. It is your move; the ball is in your court. God knocks on the door of our hearts, but we must come to Him to be saved.

Scripture Reference for the Day: "For there is one God and one mediator between God and mankind, the man Christ Jesus, who gave himself as a ransom for all people. This has now been witnessed to at the proper time." (1 Timothy 2:5, 6)

Day 80

When discussing the thousands of people who had came forward during the Billy Graham crusades, Dr. Graham confided that he didn't know how many people had true conversions. He eventually called in Dawson Trotman, the founder of a discipleship ministry called the Navigators, to help. The job of the Navigators was to follow up with and to disciple those who made a public profession of faith at the crusades.

I recall an old episode of the television series *M.A.S.H.*, where Father Mulcahy had similar concerns to those of Billy Graham. He did not know if what he was doing had any real impact on the lives of those he ministered to. Everyone in ministry has experienced this at some point. A long time ago, a godly man told me that God will never waste my time. Even though this is a true statement, I still have doubts from time to time as to whether I am having an impact.

I wrote this poem to encourage spiritual leaders, and in the process, I found myself being encouraged:

> The carpenter can see his work when the job is
>   done;
> The lawyers count their money when the case is
>   won.
> The athletes see results even when they are sore;
> All they need to do is look up at the score.
> Professional people know when they have success;
> So why should the preachers deserve any less.

But the preachers must wait to see those they
    help save;
Not knowing, who all followed the path, that
    with God's help they paved.
Sometimes I fear the pastors might feel some-
    what let down;
So I dedicate this to the preachers—the preachers
    in every town.

A plumber knows he's done his job when there
    is no leak;
And the policemen feel much better when they
    find the ones they seek.
A doctor tastes success when he saves a life;
A bachelor is fulfilled when he takes a wife.
The chef knows he is successful when people eat
    the food;
And the roughnecks sees the end result, when
    they hit the crude.
Professional people know, when they have
    success;
So why should the preachers deserve any less.
But the preachers must wait to see, those they
    help save;
Not knowing who all followed the path, that
    with God's help they paved.
Sometimes I fear the pastors might feel some-
    what let down;
So I dedicate this to the preachers—the preachers
    in every town.

Scripture Reference for the Day: "So is my word that goes out from my mouth: It will not return to me empty but will accomplish what I desire and achieve the purpose for which I sent it." (Isaiah 55:11)

Day 81

First Corinthians 3:16 says, "Do you not know that you are God's temple and that God's Spirit dwells in you?" The Bible states repeatedly that the Spirit of God lives *in* the believer.

Pretend for a moment that you are a house. Now, imagine that God has come to live in you. He begins by building you a new roof. Next, He installs new windows. Now you can see more clearly the houses that surround you. Then God paints the outside. At this point, you are looking and feeling good, as far as a house goes.

Then God goes to work on the inside. He starts tearing down your walls and dismantling your doors. This, in contrast to the new roof and windows, is not very enjoyable to you. In fact, it is a very painful experience. You do not want to go through all this pain. But God reassures you and tells you that this is necessary if He is going to put His house in order. Still, you begin to question whether you really want God changing all these things.

You know that your friends will no longer recognize you. You fear that your family will have nothing to do with you. And you know that the other houses that you once admired will reject and rebuke a house that the Lord built. However, you allow God to be God, and you embrace God's plan because you understand it is for your own good.

Now God can really get busy. He puts in new walls and new doors. He takes the trash out. Everything is made new. The new you is a beautiful thing on the inside and out. God gives you a brand-new key to your front door. He says that no other key will work. Jesus is the key. He unlocks the door of your heart so that your soul may be free to love God.

I have just described to you the spiritual process scholars call *sanctification*. God is working in you to bring you more in line with the image of Christ. No longer are you just committed to the things of God; you are learning to turn your entire life over to God. You seek to hold every thought captive to God because you dare not sin against Him. You are led by the Spirit to find new ways to glorify your Father in Heaven. And you are blessed in ways you couldn't understand previously.

Is this a description of you? If not, it can be. Seek God with all your heart and see for yourself if what I am saying is true.

Scripture Reference for the Day: "We demolish arguments and every pretension that sets itself up against the knowledge of God, and we take captive every thought to make it obedient to Christ." (2 Corinthians 10:5)

A human being is not an evolved ape as the world would have us to believe. The Bible teaches us that humanity was created in the image of God. This explains why human life is so precious to God.

That little baby in the womb has its own unique DNA. In fact, the DNA of a single cell after conception is different from that of the mother.

These tests show that this single cell is a unique human being in early stages of development. Proving once and for all, that which is in the womb is not mere tissue. This brings up the question, "How can the issue of abortion be about women's health when it threatens the existence of another human being?" If abortionists do not believe that unborn babies are human beings, then why do they harvest and sell their individual body parts? And why are so many species in the animal kingdom protected while human life is being exterminated?

When we make the decision on who gets to live or die, are we not putting ourselves in the place of God? Ronald Reagan said it best when he said, "I have noticed that everyone who is for abortion has already been born." God tells us to protect the innocent. No person is more innocent than a child in the womb. And the safest place in the world for unborn children should be their mother's womb. It is a travesty that the womb is now the most dangerous place in the world for a baby. In America we have terminated the lives of over 60 million unborn babies since 1973. If that doesn't get your attention, here is something else you may want to consider: abortion not only affects the baby and the parents, it affects countless generations of people who will never be born. I really wish this would become a talking point for pro-life advocates.

Consider hypothetically for a moment that your mother was aborted. You and your brothers and sisters would not exist. Your children and your siblings' children would cease to be. Your grand-children, your great nieces and great nephews would disappear from reality. An entire bloodline ceases to exist, when a future mother is aborted. There would be no need for a family reunion because there would be no more family. When seen from this perspective, abortion is genocide!

Most of us love our family and couldn't imagine a world without them. Many men and women who have been involved in an abortion have testified to the guilt and the pain that came from their decision. Most of them cannot help wondering what their child would be like today. And most women are never told about the possibility of future health problems caused by abortion.

But here is the good news: If you have been involved in an abortion, remember: God loves you and He will always love you. Forgiveness and healing is available through Jesus Christ. If you have always believed that abortion is a choice that women should be able to make, I hope that these facts will lead you to rethink your position.

The reason little babies in the womb have their own unique DNA is because God has a unique plan for their lives. We have a responsibility to protect all human life. The innocent human life of unborn children is no different. Babies in the womb can't take a stand or fight for their right to exist. Therefore, we must fight for them.

Scripture Reference for the Day: "Before I formed you in the womb I knew you, and before you were born I consecrated you." (Jeremiah 1:5)

Day 83

Dr. William Tolar passed away on December 29, 2018. He was a highly respected theologian, Bible historian and author. He taught at Baylor University and Southwestern Baptist Theological Seminary for 40 years. Years ago, Dr. Tolar came to speak at our Church in Tyler Texas.

As a new Christian, I was blessed to hear his sermon, based on the book he wrote, *Creation: Chance or Choice*. And I was greatly influenced by his research. Here are a few things I recall from his visit.

Our moon is the perfect size and distance from the Earth for its gravitational pull. If there was any variance in this distance, life would cease to exist on earth. The earth sits on its axis at an angle of 23.5 degrees. This is essential for life in that it allows the surface of the Earth to be properly warmed and cooled every day. The sun is the exact distance from the earth that is necessary to sustain life.

The very ecosystems God put in place for us, remains in balance, and life could not exist if they did not. The odds of these things coming together by accident are beyond astronomical. Allowing even a fractional variance in any of these areas would make life on Earth impossible.

I only gave you a couple examples that give us scientific evidence that there is a God. But there are many things necessary to Sustain life here on earth, and we have absolutely no control over any of them. Our very existence depends on all of them working together in perfect harmony.

Someone once said, "The complexity of our planet points to a deliberate Designer who not only created our universe but sustains it to this day." Even with all this evidence, there are millions of people who still oppose the concept of a Creator.

A wise man once asked, "Wouldn't it be better to live your life assuming there is a God, than to live your life assuming there isn't a God, only to find out that there is?" The truth is, men do not reject the Bible because it contradicts itself; they reject the Bible because it contradicts them. Believing in God makes perfect sense because it is common sense. Colossians 1:16 says, "For in him all things were created: things in heaven and on earth, visible and invisible, whether thrones or powers or rulers or authorities; all things have been created through him and for him."

Perhaps the most important thing we can do is to remember just how big our God really is. When we do, we will begin to understand just how foolish the theory of evolution really is.

If we were able to know God fully or to measure His abilities, we would be like God and He would cease being God to us. And the truth is, we would no longer consider God worthy of our worship.

However, we know that this will never happen. As humans, we cannot even begin to understand the depth or the magnitude of our God. Our minds and our imaginations are limited this side of heaven. Therefore, we can't even begin to scratch the surface of just how big God really is.

Earth is a million times smaller than the star God made to warm it. I recently read an article that said, "We live in a solar system one ten-millionth the diameter of our galaxy and our galaxy consists of hundreds of billions of stars. In addition, the universe has hundreds of billions of galaxies." The God of the Bible created all of this by simply speaking it into existence. Now consider again the fact that God sustains all of this. Then consider the fact that His Spirit resides in the heart of all believers and He is actively involved in the life of every one of them.

So just how big is the God of the universe? The question is unanswerable because God is immeasurable.

Scripture Reference for the Day: "I am the Alpha and the Omega, says the Lord God, who is and who was and who is to come, the Almighty." (Revelation 1:8)

My dear friend, James Dean Nations, was tragically murdered by his adopted son in June 2016. A few months earlier on April 10, I had contacted Dean to ask his permission to share something that he had written on Facebook. I explained that I wanted to include it in this book. The following is a portion of Dean's letter replying to my request.

> "I'm honored my friend. You and I lived a crazy life together for a lot of years. It warms my heart to know how we turned out… Some people are afraid to witness to others because they feel they don't have the gift of words. This is where your actions in your everyday life comes in. This is the best witness. People are always watching… God bless you my brother."

Below is the post I had asked Dean for permission to share.

> "I find myself standing in the bowels of Hell. It is so hot, so very hot. *Just a drop of water, please!* There is none. And there will never be any. I look up to Heaven and I scream for God to have mercy on my soul. I see some people I know embracing Jesus. Why? I shout. Why did I not listen to them when they told me about this man called Jesus?"

To make a point, my friend put himself in the shoes of millions of people who will not spend eternity in Heaven. Instead they will spend eternity in a place designed for Satan and his demons, a place of eternal torture.

Please don't let one of these lost souls be yours. Heed my friends warning. If you haven't worked out your salvation with the Lord, then you are missing out on the greatest gift ever offered to mankind. Do not gamble with your eternal soul. Hell is complete separation from God. On the cross, when Jesus cried out, "My God, My God, why have You forsaken Me?" He experienced the separation from God that we as sinners deserved. Jesus experienced this separation from His Father, so you and I would not have to experience eternal separation from Him.

Someone once said, "Jesus came to pay a debt He didn't owe because we owed a debt we could not pay." Jesus wants nothing more than to see you in Heaven. So if you haven't made the decision for Christ yet, do yourself a favor; make Jesus the Lord of your life today. If He is already your savior, make the decision to live the rest of your life as if you believe it. Time is of the essence. A few months ago, my dear friend Dean had no idea that he would be leaving this world. None of us know how long we have. Please, make your decision to follow Jesus today. For in Him you will find true peace. I leave you with these words from Dean Nations, "May peace be your journey."

Scripture Reference for the Day: "But God demonstrates His own love toward us, in that while we were yet sinners, Christ died for us." (Romans 5:8)

Day 85

Yesterday, I wrote about my friend Dean Nations. Afterwards, I remembered a question he asked a few years ago.

Dean asked me, "Why did I have to go through so many years of sinful regret before I finally nailed down my salvation?"

Like my friend Dean, I have also wondered why God reaches different people at different stages of life. I was an adult when I felt the need to ask Jesus into my life. Prior to this, I wandered around aimlessly with a false since of security that lasted thirty years. God's grace came to me at a time in my life when I was ready to accept it.

God's timing is definitely in sync with man's readiness to accept His truth. But I believe there is more to this than just a person's preparedness. God gives each of us a unique personalized testimony. This means that you and I can reach someone for Christ that no one else can reach.

Sometimes, I can connect with a person when others cannot. And there have been times when God had to use someone other than myself to reach a person. I believe God uses what we refer to as common ground to create an unseen bond with others. When we realize that another person has walked in our shoes we are more likely to listen to what they have to say.

Every believer has a testimony: Perhaps it will be your testimony that wins that final soul for Christ. God knows the name of the last person who will be written into the Book of Life. Wouldn't it be great to be the witness that God chose from the beginning of time to lead this person in a prayer of repentance and salvation?

The truth is, I do not want to miss any opportunity to share the gospel. I believe when I share my story, I glorify God. And that is by far the most important thing I can do with my life.

God wants you to bring honor and glory to His holy name. When you become a willing participant in the process, you will discover God's plan for your life, a plan that was put into place before you were ever born. So don't spend too much time dwelling on why you had to go through all those years of sinful regret. Instead, praise God that your name is written in the Book of Life.

Scripture Reference for the Day: "But you will receive power when the Holy Spirit comes on you; and you will be my witnesses in Jerusalem, and in all Judea and Samaria, and to the ends of the earth." (Acts 1:8)

Day 86

My first daughter was born when I was eighteen years old. I couldn't remember ever being so happy and content. On the down side, my wife was very sick and remained in the hospital bed for many days. I spent the next eight days at that hospital holding, feeding, and singing to my new baby.

During that time, baby Le'Chelle began showing signs of being sick. She died just nine days after she came into this world. To say I was devastated would be an understatement. I still cry sometimes when I think about her.

At the time, I did not have a relationship with God. However, I did believe in a God. I viewed God as a grandfather-like person with white hair and a beard who lived up in heaven. I understood Him to be *good* in every sense of the word. So I cried out to this good God that I knew very little about.

Two days before the funeral, I had what most people would describe as a nervous breakdown. I found myself sitting on the floor in my parents' walk-in closet, rocking back and forth.

I have no idea how many hours I spent in that closet. I remember praying, crying, and rocking. I remember singing and chanting about how my baby was going to come back to life. I purposely asked for the casket to remain open during the service. I did this because I truly expected Le'Chelle to start breathing on the day of the funeral.

When she didn't, I was even more devastated. I felt like God had let me down. It wasn't long after Pam came home from the hospital when I heard the words, "I want a divorce."

Years later, Pam revealed to me her reason for leaving. She said that she believed that I had lied to her. She reminded me about a red-headed woman who had lived at the same apartments we did. The lady had a miscarriage while Pam was pregnant. Pam had told me that she feared that this could happen to us. I can still remember my prideful reply, "Our baby is a "Salts" and nothing like that could ever happen to a Salts baby!" Pam felt I had lied to her, and in a way, I had. The truth is we were both very young, confused and immature. I am glad that after all we went through, and after all these years, we are still friends.

Shortly after Le'Chelle's death, Pam left for California. I was alone. Life for me was no longer worth living. I turned to alcohol and drugs to help ease the pain. But the drugs and alcohol only made things worse. I believed that my daughter was in heaven, but I did not understand the gravity of it all.

It never occurred to me that God had answered my prayer that day in my parents' closet. Nearly fifteen years after I received Jesus as my Lord and savior, my eyes were finally open to the fact that God had indeed answered my prayer to let my daughter live. Let me say it this way, "I always believed that Le'Chelle went to heaven, but it never crossed my mind that her going to heaven was an answer to my prayers."

Today, I understand that Le'Chelle is alive. She is really alive! She is more alive than you and me. Years ago, I begged God to let Le'Chelle live, and today I know she does. *She lives because Christ Jesus lives!*

Le'Chelle did not leave the land of the living to go to the land of the dying. She left the land of the dying to go to the land of the living! It took many years for me to be able to understand and to articulate this in a way that others might understand.

Perhaps this is why the lyrics to "Because He Lives" are so meaningful to me.

Because He lives, I can face tomorrow.
Because He lives, all fear is gone.
Because I know, He holds the future,
and life is worth the living just because He lives.

We have all lost loved ones and experienced the pain associated with our loss. Let today's message be encouraging to you. Trust the word of God and listen to the words of Jesus.

In John 11:25, 26, "Jesus said, "I am the resurrection and the life; he who believes in Me will live even if he dies, and everyone who lives and believes in Me will never die."

Did you know that King David also experienced the loss of a child? David spoke these words after the death of his child, "While the child was still alive, I fasted and wept. I thought, 'Who knows? The LORD may be gracious to me and let the child live. But now that he is dead, why should I go on fasting? Can I bring him back again? *I will go to him, but he will not return to me.*'" David took great comfort in knowing where his son was, and who he was with. He knew that his son was in good hands and that he would never again have to endure pain and suffering.

I found great comfort in David's words. And like so many others, I can also find comfort in a song or a poem. To this day, the lyrics to one song still comes to mind.

As you read these words consider the comfort they might give to someone you know that has experienced the loss of a son or daughter. It doesn't matter how old they were when they died. In the eyes of parents, the child will always be their little baby.

> Jesus has a rocking chair;
> He holds those precious children, with oh such
> tender care.
> He takes the place of mom and dad:
> He is the greatest parent a child could have.
> So don't worry about your children there;
> Jesus has a rocking chair.

Scripture Reference for the Day: "He will wipe away every tear from their eyes, and death shall be no more, neither shall there be mourning, nor crying, nor pain anymore, for the former things have passed away." (Revelation 21:4)

Day 87

Years ago, I had a very vivid dream. In the dream, two men were chasing me. They had guns and clubs, and somehow, I knew they were going to kill me. I don't know the reason why they wanted to kill me, but I knew I was about to die!

I ran, and I ran, and every time I thought I had eluded them, they appeared again. I could not get away from them. I remember being more desperate than I had ever been before. The chase continued until Dennis Milstead showed up. In real life, Dennis Milstead is a good friend of mine. He is a brother-in-Christ who I have spent a lot of time with. Over the years, we have served together in several outreach ministries. We have laughed together and cried together. So I was extremely happy to see him show up in my dream. In my dream Dennis walked across the street to talk to the two men. These same men who stood a head taller than me looked like little children next to Dennis. I was unable to hear what he said, but I could see everything clearly. Dennis looked like a giant compared to the men who had been chasing me. And as soon as he spoke to them they disappeared. Somehow, I knew I would never see them again. Then I woke up.

A while back, God reminded me of this dream, and He also revealed to me that my dream had come true and that the demons that once chased me are long gone. I believe God used this dream to show me how powerful intercessory prayer can be and just how vital prayer warriors like Dennis Milstead are. As a prayer warrior, Dennis intercedes in the spiritual realm on the behalf of others. I thank God for Dennis and all the other prayer warriors of this world.

One thing I didn't mention is that Dennis has been in a wheelchair his entire life. For him, the wheelchair is his pulpit. During a time when I was really struggling with an addiction to alcohol, I shared with Dennis the horrors of what I was going through. And Dennis has prayed on my behalf for many years. Today, the demons that once chased and tormented me are gone. I hope you have a prayer warrior like Dennis to intercede for you. If you don't have one, make it a priority to find a prayer partner who you know will be faithful to pray for you. And someday you will look back, and you will see how their prayers made a difference in your life.

Scripture Reference for the Day: "And pray in the Spirit on all occasions with all kinds of prayers and requests. With this in mind, be alert and always keep on praying for all the Lord's people." (Ephesians 6:18)

Day 88

A father took his son into the forest and blindfolded him. Then he explained to his son that he had to sit alone on a stump. He was to sit there all night in complete darkness. He said, "You must not remove the blindfold until you feel the rays of the morning sun on your skin." He was not allowed to cry out for help or to move from where he was. In addition, he was warned that he could never speak about his experience to anybody. The last words the son heard from his father before he left was, "If you do as I say, and you survive until morning, you will no longer be considered a boy; you will have become a man."

The boy was terrified to say the least. He could hear all kinds of noises and he was certain that wild animals were all around him. He believed that he might be killed, but for him, it was worth it. This was, after all, the custom of his tribe. For his people, this was the only path to manhood. So he sat still without making a sound the entire night. When the night was over, and he could feel the warmth of the sun on his face, he slowly began to remove the blindfold.

When he did, he discovered his father sitting on a stump next to him. His father had been there to protect him the entire night.

If you are a child of God, you are never truly alone. Even when you are unaware of it, your heavenly Father is next to you, watching over you and protecting you.

Scripture Reference for the Day: "The LORD is near to those who have a broken heart and saves such as have a contrite spirit." (Psalm 34:18)

Day 89

We don't necessarily need more faith to accomplish the will of God. What we need is the kind of faith that leads to obedience. Faith like this cannot be found in material things; this kind of faith is found only in Jesus Christ. The measure of a person's faith is in direct proportion to the time they spend with God. It is about who your faith is in, that makes all the difference.

For an entire week, the storm raged. It was a winter storm of biblical proportions. David had a young son who was very ill. His life depended upon his daily dose of medication. It happened that his little boy was completely out of his medication when the storm subsided. David knew he had to drive into town to get the medicine that his boy needed. When he got to the bridge on his way to town, he noticed that it had collapsed under the weight of the ice. He also noted that the lake had frozen over.

Understanding that his son's health depended on him getting to town, he got out of his vehicle and began pressing on the ice. He needed to know if it could support his weight.

Since he was unsure of the thickness of the ice, he began to cross gingerly on his hands and knees. When he was about halfway across, he heard a motor running. Looking over his shoulder, he noticed a truck about fifty yards away. David watched as the truck drove across the ice and proceeded toward town.

Obviously, the man in the truck had more faith in the ability of the ice to sustain weight than David did. The good news is they both made it across.

Our faith is only as good as the object in which it is placed. If the object is worthy of our faith, it will sustain us even when our faith is weak. No one is worthier of our faith than Jesus Christ. When you place your trust in Him, you can be sure that He will carry you safely to the other side.

Scripture Reference for the Day: "Because you have so little faith. Truly I tell you, if you have faith as small as a mustard seed, you can say to this mountain, 'Move from here to there,' and it will move. Nothing will be impossible for you." (Matthew 17:20)

Day 90

A young man had committed murder and was on death row. His mother was a woman of faith who prayed for her son every day. She sent letter after letter to the governor of her state, begging him to stop the execution of her son. For her, life in prison seemed better than death. The governor was a Christian man, and he knew that the penalty her son had received was justified.

Based on the horrible crimes that were committed, he said that he could not in good conscience overrule the judge. But the boy's mother persisted. One day, she was able to slip past the governor's secretary.

She barged into the governor's office and threw herself face first on the floor. She crawled on her knees to the governor, grabbed hold of his legs, and begged him to have mercy on her son. The governor said, "I am not making any promises, but I will go talk to your son."

The next day he went to the prison to visit the young man. When they were alone, he asked the young man if he knew Jesus. To his amazement, he was ignored. So he tried another tactic. He asked, "Do you have any idea how much your mother loves you?" And still the young man said nothing. For ten minutes, he tried in vain to get a response. Then he gave up and asked the guard to open the door of the cell.

As the door slammed shut, the guard said, "Thank you for coming, Governor." The governor walked down the hall and left. Startled, the young man jumped up and yelled for the guard. "Did I hear you say, that was the Governor?" When the guard confirmed to him that it was indeed the governor, the prisoner became angry.

His cursing and screaming could be heard in nearly every cell. Then he started mumbling repeatedly, "He was the only person who could change my sentence. No one else has the authority to spare my life, and I wouldn't even talk to him."

That following week he was standing in the gallows. As the rope was placed around his neck, the executioner could hear him still mumbling, "He came to me and I ignored him. He was right beside me in my cell. He was the only person who could do anything about this, and I wouldn't even talk to Him."

Friends don't be someone who refuses to talk to Jesus. Jesus is talking to you right now. Perhaps you have never really trusted Jesus with your life. Today, Jesus is giving you another chance to live for Him. Do you trust Jesus enough to give your life to Him? Trusting Jesus in this way, means we can no longer leave our options open. It's all or nothing.

Don't miss this opportunity to draw near to Jesus. The Bible says, "Today is the day of salvation!" Don't be like that young man on death row. Don't gamble with your soul. No one wants to spend eternity in a lake of fire mumbling, "Jesus came to me, He was right beside me. He was the only person who could change my sentence, He was the only One who could have delivered me from this place called Hell, and I wouldn't even talk to Him."

Scripture Reference for the Day: "Seek the LORD while He may be found; Call upon Him while He is near." (Isaiah 55:6)

CPSIA information can be obtained
at www.ICGtesting.com
Printed in the USA
FSHW021903310120